Top Executive Compensation: 1990 Edition

by Elizabeth R. Arreglado

Contents

TABLES

MANUFACTURING

AEROSPACE

COMPUTER HARDWARE AND OFFICE EQUIPMENT

Author's Acknowledgments

Analytical programming was provided by Diana Benenati under the direction of E. Kay Worrell, Director, Survey Research Center. Charts were prepared by Chuck N. Tow, Chief Chartist. Charles Peck, Senior Research Associate, assisted with the interpretation of the data.

About the Author

Elizabeth R. Arreglado is Research Associate, Corporate Practices Program. She plans and conducts the Board's research on corporate compensation programs.

From the President

Although 1989 was a year of overall expansion of the U.S. economy, profit performance was erratic with some industry sectors registering declines from 1988 levels. An atmosphere of turbulence prevailed as many companies continued to restructure their businesses to meet the fierce pressures of global competition. The view from the end of the decade is of a dubious past year and an uncertain future. Executive compensation, with its reliance on incentives tied to business performance, is particularly sensitive to such conditions, and there was considerable variation in the pattern of 1989 executive compensation among industries.

This study reports the average total current compensation (salary and bonus) for 1989 of the five highest paid executives in 645 companies representing eight major industry groups. Also covered are long-term compensation devices, including restricted stock awards, performance unit/share plans and stock option plans. These arrangements are intended to reward top executives for the performance of the business over a period of years and have become an increasingly prominent part of executive compensation.

The report is designed to ensure maximum clarity and ease of interpretation. Using it, a company can compare the pay of its highest paid executives quickly and easily with their counterparts in the same or different industries and size categories. It was made possible by the several hundred companies that participated in the survey. We appreciate their generous contribution of time and effort.

PRESTON TOWNLEY
President and CEO

Executive Summary

The 1989 compensation of the five highest-paid executives in each of 645 surveyed companies in eight major types of businesses is analyzed in this report. The major focus is on 1989 total current compensation, defined as base salary paid in 1989 and bonus earned for 1989 company performance. Using this report, a company can compare the 1989 compensation of its top-paid executives with that of their counterparts in companies in similar or different sizes and types of businesses.

The report also describes the incidence of, and trends in, four important elements of the executive compensation package: annual bonus plans, long-term performance plans, stock option plans, and restricted stock plans. For stock options, the size of option grants during 1989 is shown, as well as the net gain for options exercised during 1989. For restricted stock plans, the size of grants during 1989 is reported. The size of payouts during 1989 is given for long-term performance plans, and the size of contingent awards made under these plans during the year is also reported.

Pay Trends

Compared with 1988, 1989 total current compensation (salary and bonus) was higher in all the industry categories surveyed. Total current compensation increased 12.6 percent in trade, 11.6 percent in utilities, 10.7 percent in insurance, 5.9 percent in manufacturing, 4.3 percent in commercial banking, 2.0 percent in energy, and 1.8 percent in diversified service.

Salaries rose in 1989 in each type of business. The increase was 10.2 percent in commercial banking, 9.4 percent in insurance, 8.8 percent in both manufacturing and trade, 8.0 percent in utilities, 6.3 percent in energy, and 4.9 percent in diversified service. There was insufficient data to show a pay trend for communications.

Median CEO total current compensation was the highest in manufacturing at $700,000. Median CEO compensation in the other seven industries were: energy, $680,000; communications, $629,000; trade, $520,000; diversified service, $510,000; commercial banking, $479,000; insurance, $463,000; and utilities, $440,000.

A survey of salary increase budgets conducted in April and May 1990 for all salaried employees show median budgets of 5.0 percent for nonexempt and exempt employees, and 5.5 percent for executives for 1990. Projected 1991 salary increase budgets for both nonexempts and executives are the same at 5.0 percent and 5.5 percent, respectively. However, the median budget for exempt employees is expected to rise to 5.5 percent.

Annual Bonus Plans

Annual bonuses are now virtually universal in all industries except utilities. And they are approaching this level in utilities; 87 percent report such plans, compared with 36 percent five years ago.

The size of the median bonus award for the CEO, as a percentage of salary, is lowest in utilities and commercial banking; 35 and 40 percent, respectively. Trade and insurance show very similar patterns at 47 and 49 percent, respectively. Communications companies paid a median bonus of 50 percent, while diversified service companies paid a median bonus of 55 percent. Energy and manufacturing companies were the highest payers, each with a median CEO bonus of 60 percent.

Restricted Stock Plans

Under these plans, companies make outright awards of restricted shares, which are often subject to forfeiture until they are "earned out" over a stipulated period of continued employment. A significant minority of companies in each type of business have a plan for awards of restricted stock to top executives: energy companies,

46 percent; banks, 41 percent; manufacturing, 39 percent; diversified service, 37 percent; utilities, 30 percent; trade, 29 percent; stock insurance companies, 28 percent; and communications, 25 percent.

During 1989, the median *award* to the five highest-paid executives as a group ranged from a high of 230 percent of salary in diversified service to a low of 26 percent in utilities.

Long-Term Performance Plans

A minority of companies in each industry group have long-term performance plans. Under these plans, top executives are given a contingent award of shares or units at the beginning of a performance period; the payment of these awards is determined by how closely specified corporate financial targets are met during a three-, four-, or five-year performance period. Such plans are most prevalent in manufacturing, 41 percent, and communications, 38 percent. Thirty-three percent of the surveyed utilities have long-term performance plans, as do 32 percent of trade. Long-term plans are found in 27 percent of both energy and insurance companies. They are least frequent in commercial banking (24 percent) and diversified service (23 percent).

During 1989, the median contingent *award* to the five highest-paid executives as a group ranged from 83 percent of salary in diversified service to 32 percent in utilities. The median *payment* for 1989 ranged from 51 percent of salary among diversified service companies to 27 percent among insurance companies.

Stock Option Plans

The majority of companies in all industry categories have stock option plans, except in utilities where 48 percent have such plans. Eighty-eight percent of the surveyed communications companies have them, as do 84 percent of the manufacturing companies, 81 percent of the energy companies, 77 percent of the trade com-

panies, 76 percent of the stock insurance companies, 72 percent of the banks, and 67 percent of the diversified service companies.

The median stock option grant made in 1989 to the five highest-paid executives as a group ranged from the equivalent of 100 to 184 percent of base salary, depending on the type of business. The median net gain for options exercised during 1989 ranged from a high of 77 percent of salary in energy firms to a low of 26 percent in commercial banking.

Method

Information for this report was collected during April and May 1990. Questionnaires were mailed to 2,749 U.S. companies. Those surveyed were medium to large manufacturers (sales of approximately $100 million or more) and companies of comparable size in seven other industry categories. The survey information was supplemented with publicly available data from corporate reports.

Usable information was collected from 645 companies in eight industry categories. The 645 respondents were distributed by industry category as follows:

Manufacturing companies (291)

Utilities, including gas, electric, water, and telecommunications (79)

Commercial banks (71)

Health, life, and property and casualty insurance companies (60)

Diversified service companies, including computer services, construction/design/engineering, health care, hotel/restaurant/entertainment, real estate, and transportation (57)

Energy and natural resources companies (37)

Wholesale and retail trade companies (34)

Communications companies, including broadcasting and printing and publishing (16)

Introduction

This report is primarily an analysis of the 1989 compensation of the five highest-paid executives in each of 645 companies (see box on "Method"). The major emphasis is on base salary *paid* in 1989 and the bonus *earned* for 1989 company performance, regardless of when paid. Total current compensation is the sum of the two. The report also describes the prevalence of and trends in four major forms of executive incentive compensation: annual bonus plans, restricted stock plans, long-term performance plans, and stock option plans.

Pay Trends

The change in CEO total current compensation from 1988 to 1989 is given in Table 1 below. This is the median change for the *function* in those companies that furnished data in both years. The *individuals* in the CEO function were not necessarily the same in both years. The same information with respect to salary is shown in Table 2.

As an indicator of future salary increases, companies were asked during April and May 1990 to provide the 1990 salary increase budget and the 1991 anticipated salary increase budget for their executive, exempt and nonexempt populations. The results are shown in Table 3 for all industries as a group and separately for those industries for which the data were sufficient to allow individual analysis.

Table 1: CEO Total Current Compensation Change, 1989 over 1988

Industry Category*	Number of Companies	Median Change
Trade	19	12.6%
Utilities	55	11.6
Insurance	43	10.7
Manufacturing	139	5.9
Commercial Banking	36	4.3
Energy	24	2.0
Diversified service	29	1.8

Table 2: CEO Salary Change, 1989 over 1988

Industry Category*	Number of Companies	Median Change
Commercial Banking	36	10.2%
Insurance	43	9.4
Manufacturing	139	8.8
Trade	19	8.8
Utilities	55	8.0
Energy	24	6.3
Diversified service	29	4.9

*Insufficient data for Communications.

Table 3: Salary Increase Budgets, 1990 and 1991

Type of Business	1990		Estimated for 1991	
	Number of Companies*	Median	Number of Companies*	Median
ALL INDUSTRIES				
Nonexempt	499	5.0%	361	5.0%
Exempt	516	5.0	374	5.5
Executive	478	5.5	350	5.5
COMMERCIAL BANKING				
Nonexempt	70	5.0	50	5.0
Exempt	70	5.1	50	5.3
Executive	62	5.3	47	5.0
DIVERSIFIED SERVICE				
Nonexempt	36	5.5	31	5.5
Exempt	37	5.5	32	5.6
Executive	36	5.7	31	5.8
INSURANCE				
Nonexempt	58	5.5	43	5.5
Exempt	58	5.5	43	5.5
Executive	56	5.5	42	5.9
MANUFACTURING				
Nonexempt	185	5.0	141	5.0
Exempt	189	5.0	146	5.3
Executive	181	5.5	139	5.5
TRADE				
Nonexempt	28	5.0	20	5.0
Exempt	28	5.0	20	5.0
Executive	26	5.0	19	5.0
UTILITIES				
Nonexempt	70	5.0	46	5.0
Exempt	77	5.0	50	5.0
Executive	66	5.5	44	5.5

* Other industry groups are included in totals but not shown separately because of small samples.

Executive Incentive Compensation

The four major forms of executive incentive compensation are:

Annual Bonus: Generally, a percentage of profits is used to create a fund that is apportioned among the eligible executives based on individual contributions to profitability.

Restricted Stock: Shares of company stock are awarded to executives and are subject to restrictions as to sale or transfer, usually for three to five years. Additional restrictions often call for forfeiture if the executive terminates employment during the restricted period.

Long-Term Performance Plans: Under these plans, executives are awarded contingent grants of cash (long-term performance *units*) or stock (long-term performance *shares*). The payment of the award usually depends on the achievement of three- to five-year financial performance goals.

Stock Options: These arrangements provide executives a right to purchase shares of company stock at a fixed price over a stated period of time. "Incentive stock options" (ISOs) meet Internal Revenue Code requirements, while "nonqualified stock options" do not. An option plan may allow "stock swaps" where previously acquired shares are used to exercise an option. "Stock appreciation rights" (SARs) may be attached to stock options. The SAR gives an optionee, in lieu of exercising the stock option in whole or in part, the right to receive an amount equal to the appreciation in the stock price since the date of grant.

To indicate trends in the incidence of these plans, the number reported in the 1990 survey is compared with the number reported in the 1985 survey. A five-year span is believed to be a good indicator. It should be noted that while the companies in the two surveys are not identical, they remain relatively constant.

Table 4: Prevalence of Annual Bonus Plans

Industry Category	Total Companies (May, 1990)	With Bonus Plan Number (May, 1990)	With Bonus Plan Percent (May, 1990)	Percent With Bonus Plan (May, 1985)
Communications	16	16	100%	*
Diversified service	57	55	97	*
Energy	37	36	97	*
Trade	34	33	97	81%
Manufacturing	291	276	95	92
Commercial banking	71	65	92	81
Insurance	60	55	92	67
Utilities	79	69	87	36

* Data not available.

Table 5: Prevalence of Bonus Awards

Industry Category	Total Plans (1989)	Percent that Paid Bonus (1989)	Percent that Paid Bonus (1988*)
Trade	33	100%	96%
Insurance	55	93	98
Utilities	69	93	95
Manufacturing	276	92	97
Diversified service	55	91	100
Communications	16	88	89
Commercial banking	65	86	98
Energy	36	86	96

* From Top Executive Compensation: 1989 Edition

Table 6: Median CEO Bonus Awards for 1989

Industry Category	Number of CEOS	Percent of Salary
Energy	24	60%
Manufacturing	170	60
Diversified service	43	55
Communications	8	50
Insurance	49	49
Trade	28	47
Commercial banking	54	40
Utilities	60	35

Table 7: Prevalence of Restricted Stock Plans

		May, 1990		May, 1985
	Total	With Restricted Stock		Percent with
Industry Category	Companies	Number	Percent	Restricted Stock
Energy	37	17	46%	*
Commercial banking	71	29	41	12%
Maufacturing	291	112	39	23
Diversified service	57	21	37	*
Utilities	79	24	30	5
Trade	34	10	29	13
Insurance: stock	25	7	28	13
Communications	16	4	25	*

* Data not available.

Table 8: Median Restricted Stock Awards for 1989 to The Five Highest-Paid Executives as a Group

Industry Category*	Number of Companies	Number of Executives	Median (Percent of Salary)
Diversified service	8	31	230%
Energy	6	24	47
Manufacturing	54	219	45
Insurance: stock	5	21	38
Commercial banking	8	32	35
Trade	6	30	33
Utilities	12	48	26

* Insufficient data for Communications.

Table 9: Prevalence of Long-Term Performance Plans

		May, 1990		May, 1985
	Total	With Long-term Performance Plans		Percent with Long-term
Industry Category	Companies	Number	Percent	Performance Plans
Manufacturing	291	120	41%	37%
Communications	16	6	38	*
Utilities	79	26	33	18
Trade	34	11	32	22
Energy	37	10	27	*
Insurance	60	16	27	20
Commercial banking	71	17	24	21
Diversified service	57	13	23	*

* Data not available.

Table 10: Types of Long-Term Performance Plans

		Number and Percent of Plans by Type					
		Both Unit and Share Plans		Only Unit Plan		Only Share Plan	
Industry Category	Total Plans	Number	Percent	Number	Percent	Number	Percent
Manufacturing	120	8	7%	71	59%	41	34%
Utilities	26	2	8	10	39	14	54
Commercial banking	17	3	18	10	59	4	24
Insurance	16	—	—	13	81	3	19
Diversified service	13	1	8	9	69	3	23
Trade	11	1	9	3	27	7	64
Energy	10	1	10	4	40	5	50
Communications	6	—	—	6	100	—	—

Table 11: Median Long-Term Performance Awards for 1989 To The Five Highest-Paid Executives as a Group

Industry Category*	Number of Companies	Number of Executives	Median (Percent of Salary)
Diversified service	7	33	83%
Trade	5	19	76
Energy	4	17	69
Manufacturing	50	240	50
Commercial banking	9	36	40
Insurance	5	25	40
Utilities	15	69	32

* Insufficient data for Communications.

Table 12: Median Long-Term Performance Payments for 1989 To the Five Highest-Paid Executives as a Group

Industry Category*	Number of Companies	Number of Executives	Median (Percent of Salary)
Diversified service	6	27	51%
Manufacturing	48	213	48
Utilities	11	52	40
Commercial banking	9	38	35
Energy	5	23	31
Trade	6	24	31
Insurance	13	60	27

* Insufficient data for Communications.

Table 13: Prevalence of Stock Option Plans

Industry Category	May, 1990 Total Companies	With Stock Option Plan Number	With Stock Option Plan Percent	May, 1985 Percent with Stock Option Plan
Communications	16	14	88%	*
Manufacturing	291	243	84	82%
Energy	37	30	81	*
Trade	34	26	77	71
Insurance: stock	25	19	76	50
Commercial banking	71	51	72	57
Diversified service	57	38	67	*
Utilities	79	38	48	20

*Data not available.

Table 14: Types of Options

Industry Category	Total Responses	Both ISO and Nonqualifed Number	Both ISO and Nonqualifed Percent	Only ISO Number	Only ISO Percent	Only Nonqualified Number	Only Nonqualified Percent
Manufacturing	243	183	75%	11	5%	49	20%
Commercial banking	50	36	72	5	10	9	18
Diversified service . .	38	23	61	3	8	12	32
Utilities	37	28	76	—	—	9	24
Energy	30	21	70	1	3	8	27
Trade	25	17	68	2	8	6	24
Insurance: stock	18	10	56	3	17	5	28
Communications . . .	14	11	79	—	—	3	21

Table 15: 1989 Stock Option Grants

Industry Category	Companies with Stock Option Plan	Granted Options in 1989 Number	Granted Options in 1989 Percent
Trade	26	21	81%
Insurance: stock	19	15	79
Commercial banking	51	38	75
Diversified service	38	26	68
Energy	30	20	67
Manufacturing	243	139	57
Utilities	38	21	55
Communications	14	6	43

Table 16: 1989 Stock Option Grants by Type

Industry Category	Total Responses	Both ISO and Nonqualifed Number	Both ISO and Nonqualifed Percent	ISO Only Number	ISO Only Percent	Nonqualified Only Number	Nonqualified Only Percent
Manufacturing	134	32	24%	13	10%	89	66%
Commercial banking	36	8	22	6	17	22	61
Diversified service	25	5	20	4	16	16	64
Utilities	21	2	10	1	5	18	86
Trade	20	3	15	3	15	14	70
Energy	19	3	16	2	11	14	74
Insurance: stock	15	3	20	3	20	9	60
Communications	6	—	—	1	17	5	83

Table 17: Incentive Stock Options with Stock Swap— Stock Appreciation Rights

Industry Category	ISO Plans	With Stock Swap		With SAR	
		Number	Percent	Number	Percent
Manufacturing	194	96	50%	57	29%
Commercial banking	41	28	68	21	51
Utilities	28	21	75	17	61
Diversified service . .	26	17	65	12	46
Energy	22	16	73	12	55
Trade	19	14	74	5	26
Insurance: stock . . .	13	9	69	7	54
Communications . . .	11	5	46	1	9

Table 18: Nonqualified Options with Stock Swap— Stock Appreciation Rights

Industry Category	Nonqualified Options	With Stock Swap		With SAR	
		Number	Percent	Number	Percent
Manufacturing	232	113	49%	71	31%
Commercial banking .	45	32	71	19	42
Utilities	37	27	73	20	54
Diversified service . . .	35	23	66	13	37
Energy	29	18	62	18	62
Trade	23	14	61	6	26
Insurance: stock	15	8	53	8	53
Communications	14	6	43	1	7

Table 19: Size of 1989 Stock Option Grants To The Five Highest-Paid Executives as a Group

Industry Category*	Number of Companies	Number of Executives	Size of Grant (Percent of Salary)		
			Median	Middle 50% Range	
				Low	High
Diversified service	20	89	184%	100%	292%
Energy	20	89	140	60	256
Manufacturing	123	572	123	71	228
Trade	17	75	117	56	240
Utilities	19	92	115	68	209
Insurance: stock	12	59	101	79	156
Commercial banking . . .	35	155	100	60	155

*Insuffecent data for Communications.

Table 20: Gains at Exercise in 1989 of the Five Highest-Paid Executives as a Group

Industry Category*	Number of Companies	Number of Executives	Dollars			Percent of Salary		
			Median	Middle 50% Range		Median	Middle 50% Range	
				Low	High		Low	High
Energy	12	34	$288,000	$107,000	$515,000	77%	30%	116%
Diversified service	10	29	197,000	61,000	772,000	45	28	254
Manufacturing	70	202	169,000	54,000	384,000	51	21	97
Trade	10	30	145,000	86,000	517,000	76	45	221
Insurance: stock	7	19	142,000	55,000	694,000	41	18	152
Utilities	11	33	109,000	73,000	275,000	52	22	93

* Insufficient data for Communications.

Compensation by Industry Category

The balance of the report contains the information listed below for each of the eight major industry categories and for 12 manufacturing subcategories.

- Distribution of companies according to size;
- Median, low, and high of middle 50 percent range for total current compensation and salary;
- Regression formulas for total current compensation and salary;
- Charts showing regression lines measuring the relationship between total current compensation and company size; and
- Total current compensation and salary of the second through fifth highest-paid executives as a percentage of CEO's pay.

Each major industry section also contains an analysis relating bonus awards to company size and a table showing the size of bonus awards for each of the five executives, with the exception of communications, where data were insufficient for analysis. Life insurance and property and casualty insurance are analyzed in separate sections.

Executive Pay and Company Size

The regression line charts and the regression formulas are based on the generally accepted belief that there is a positive correlation between company size and executive pay. The CEO of a large company is paid more than the CEO of a small company because the large company CEO has a more difficult and demanding job.

The regression lines on the charts measure the general relationship between total current compensation and company size. The lines can be used for determining the average compensation of executives according to company size. For greater precision, the regression formulas can be used.

(See the Appendix on page 71 for an explanation of how to use the formulas.)

Manufacturing

Chart 1: Total Current Compensation of the Five Highest-Paid Executives, by Company Sales

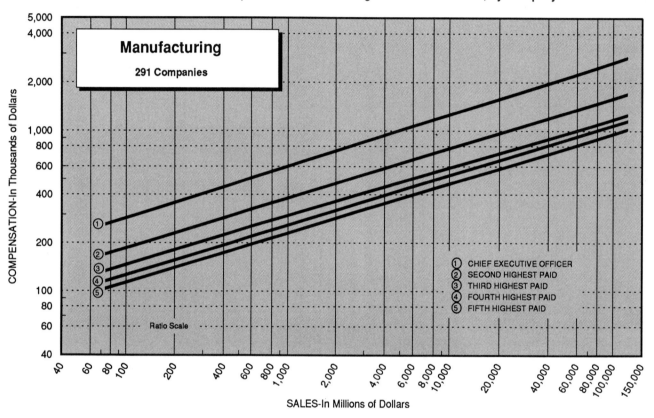

Manufacturing

291 Companies

① CHIEF EXECUTIVE OFFICER
② SECOND HIGHEST PAID
③ THIRD HIGHEST PAID
④ FOURTH HIGHEST PAID
⑤ FIFTH HIGHEST PAID

COMPENSATION-In Thousands of Dollars

SALES-In Millions of Dollars

Ratio Scale

Table 21: 1989 Sales Volume

1989 Sales	Companies	
	Number	Percent
$5 billion and over	68	23%
2-4,999 billion	53	18
1-1,999 billion	48	17
500-999 million	49	17
300-499 million	32	11
200-299 million	27	9
199 million and under	14	5
TOTAL	291	100%

Median	Middle 50% Range	
	Low	High
$1.4 billion	$485 million	$4.3 billion

Table 22: 1989 Total Current Compensation

Compensation Rank	Median	Middle 50% Range	
		Low	High
CEO	$700,000	$450,000	$1,060,000
Second highest	422,000	285,000	639,000
Third highest	329,000	232,000	491,000
Fourth highest	288,000	202,000	445,000
Fifth highest	257,000	176,000	372,000

Table 23: 1989 Total Current Compensation Regression Formula

Compensation Rank	Formula	r^2
CEO	log Y = 1.8070 + 0.3230 log X	61%
Second highest	log Y = 1.6320 + 0.3140 log X	62
Third highest	log Y = 1.5880 + 0.2950 log X	64
Fourth highest	log Y = 1.4760 + 0.3110 log X	69
Fifth highest	log Y = 1.4310 + 0.3100 log X	70

Table 24: Total Current Compensation as a Percentage of CEO's Total Current Compensation*

Compensation Rank	Median	Middle 50% Range	
		Low	High
Second highest	64%	54%	75%
Third highest	50	42	58
Fourth highest	43	37	51
Fifth highest	38	33	45

* Please note that for all tables showing this relationship, the percentages are not based on the preceding table showing the median and the middle 50 percent range of total current compensation.

Table 25: 1989 Salary

Compensation Rank	Median	Middle 50% Range	
		Low	High
CEO	$463,000	$338,000	$610,000
Second highest	290,000	210,000	395,000
Third highest	231,000	172,000	306,000
Fourth highest	207,000	158,000	278,000
Fifth highest	195,000	139,000	255,000

Table 26: 1989 Salary Regression Formula

Compensation Rank	Formula	r^2
CEO	log Y = 1.8580 + 0.2480 log X	62%
Second highest	log Y = 1.6280 + 0.2580 log X	65
Third highest	log Y = 1.5950 + 0.2400 log X	63
Fourth highest	log Y = 1.5100 + 0.2510 log X	69
Fifth highest	log Y = 1.4950 + 0.2430 log X	67

Table 27: Salary as a Percentage of CEO's Salary*

Compensation Rank	Median	Middle 50% Range	
		Low	High
Second highest	65%	57%	75%
Third highest	52	45	59
Fourth highest	46	40	52
Fifth highest	43	37	49

* Please note that for all tables showing this relationship, the percentages are not based on the preceding table showing the median and middle 50 percent range of salary.

Table 28: 1989 Bonus Awards (as Percent of Salary), by Company Size

Executive	Sales Volume		
	Middle 50% Range		
	Low	Median	High
	$485 Million	$1.4 Billion	$4.3 Billion
CEO			
1989 Bonus	47%	57%	69%
Salary	$330,000	$432,000	$574,000
Second Highest			
1989 Bonus	45%	53%	63%
Salary	$206,000	$273,000	$368,000
Third Highest			
1989 Bonus	44%	52%	60%
Salary	$168,000	$219,000	$289,000
Fourth Highest			
1989 Bonus	39%	48%	58%
Salary	$152,000	$197,000	$260,000
Fifth Highest			
1989 Bonus	33%	43%	54%
Salary	$138,000	$180,000	$237,000

Table 29: 1989 Bonus Awards

1989 Bonus Awards (Percent of Salary)	CEOS		Second Highest Paid		Third Highest Paid		Fourth Highest Paid		Fifth Highest Paid	
	Number	Percent	Number	Percent	Number	Percent	Number	Percent	Number	Percent
100% or more	34	20%	24	14%	26	15%	19	11%	17	10%
90-99	4	2	6	3	4	2	6	3	3	2
80-89	16	9	12	7	6	3	10	6	12	7
70-79	14	8	13	7	16	9	8	5	6	4
60-69	21	12	19	11	12	7	12	7	13	8
50-59	17	10	25	14	26	15	23	13	18	11
40-49	25	15	28	16	25	14	37	21	32	19
30-39	15	9	18	10	32	18	24	14	25	15
20-29	14	8	17	10	15	9	21	12	23	14
10-19	6	4	8	5	10	6	13	7	13	8
Less than 10%	4	2	5	3	5	3	4	2	8	5
Total	170	100%	175	100%	177	100%	177	100%	170	100%
Median Bonus	60%		54%		50%		47%		43%	
Middle 50% Range	41 – 87%		36 – 78%		34 – 74%		33 – 68%		29 – 65%	

Individual Manufacturing Industries

Aerospace

Chart 2: Total Current Compensation of the Five Highest-Paid Executives, by Company Sales

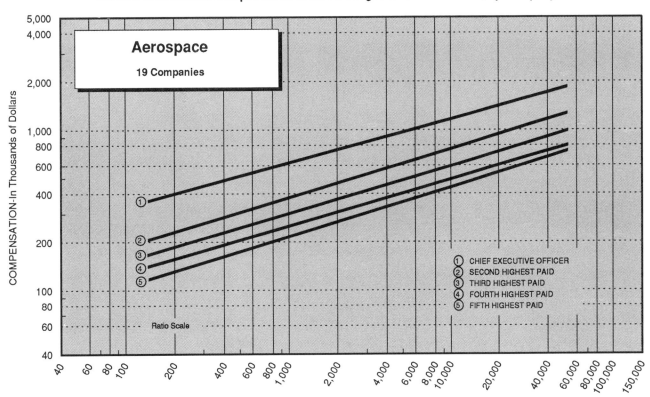

SALES-In Millions of Dollars

Table 30: 1989 Sales Volume

1989 Sales	Companies	
	Number	Percent
$5 billion and over	10	53%
2-4,999 billion	3	16
1-1,999 billion	3	16
500-999 million	—	—
300-499 million	2	11
299 million and under	1	5
Total	19	100%

Median	Middle 50% Range	
	Low	High
$5.8 billion	$1.1 billion	$12.5 billion

Table 31: 1989 Total Current Compensation

Compensation Rank	Median	Middle 50% Range	
		Low	High
CEO	$851,000	$589,000	$1,356,000
Second highest	650,000	305,000	886,000
Third highest	457,000	280,000	686,000
Fourth highest	370,000	255,000	592,000
Fifth highest	362,000	178,000	570,000

Table 32: 1989 Total Current Compensation Regression Formula

Compensation Rank	Formula	r^2
CEO	$\log Y = 1.9600 + 0.2780 \log X$	49%
Second highest	$\log Y = 1.6580 + 0.3070 \log X$	59
Third highest	$\log Y = 1.6140 + 0.2880 \log X$	53
Fourth highest	$\log Y = 1.5280 + 0.2910 \log X$	65
Fifth highest	$\log Y = 1.3730 + 0.3200 \log X$	71

Table 33: Total Current Compensation as a Percentage of CEO's Total Current Compensation

Compensation Rank	Median	Middle 50% Range	
		Low	High
Second highest	67%	55%	77%
Third highest	50	43	56
Fourth highest	42	37	46
Fifth highest	38	34	42

Table 34: 1989 Salary

Compensation Rank	Median	Middle 50% Range	
		Low	High
CEO	$571,000	$388,000	$730,000
Second highest	337,000	210,000	455,000
Third highest	245,000	184,000	360,000
Fourth highest	225,000	190,000	317,000
Fifth highest		Insufficient data	

Table 35: 1989 Salary Regression Formula

Compensation Rank	Formula	r^2
CEO	$\log Y = 1.9560 + 0.2180 \log X$	68%
Second highest	$\log Y = 1.6410 + 0.2520 \log X$	70
Third highest	$\log Y = 1.6430 + 0.2200 \log X$	65
Fourth highest	$\log Y = 1.6220 + 0.2100 \log X$	75
Fifth highest	$\log Y = 1.5000 + 0.2370 \log X$	78

Table 36: Salary as a Percentage of CEO's Salary

Compensation Rank	Median	Middle 50% Range	
		Low	High
Second highest	66%	55%	74%
Third highest	50	43	55
Fourth highest	42	39	50
Fifth highest	40	37	49

Computer Hardware and Office Equipment

Chart 3: Total Current Compensation of the Five Highest-Paid Executives, by Company Sales

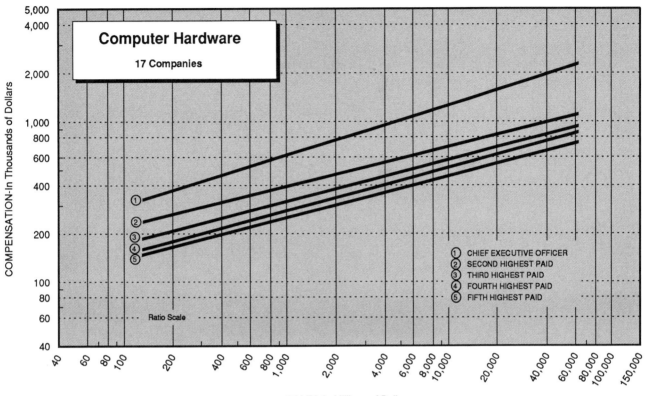

Table 37: 1989 Sales Volume

1989 Sales	Companies	
	Number	Percent
$5 billion and over	6	35%
2-4,999 billion	2	12
1-1,999 billion	4	24
500-999 million	1	6
300-499 million	2	12
200-299 million	1	6
199 million and under	1	6
Total	17	100%

Median	Middle 50% Range	
	Low	High
$1.8 billion	$785 million	$10.1 billion

Table 38: 1989 Total Current Compensation

Compensation Rank	Median	Middle 50% Range	
		Low	High
CEO	$781,000	$479,000	$1,290,000
Second highest	422,000	339,000	734,000
Third highest	320,000	283,000	652,000
Fourth highest	289,000	257,000	574,000
Fifth highest	274,000	214,000	512,000

Table 39: 1989 Total Current Compensation Regression Formula

Compensation Rank	Formula	r^2
CEO	$\log Y = 1.8410 + 0.3150 \log X$	63%
Second highest	$\log Y = 1.8570 + 0.2460 \log X$	64
Third highest	$\log Y = 1.7300 + 0.2580 \log X$	74
Fourth highest	$\log Y = 1.6130 + 0.2760 \log X$	75
Fifth highest	$\log Y = 1.6000 + 0.2660 \log X$	69

Table 40: Total Current Compensation as a Percentage of CEO's Total Current Compensation

Compensation Rank	Median	Middle 50% Range	
		Low	High
Second highest	63%	46%	81%
Third highest	52	38	63
Fourth highest	45	34	55
Fifth highest	44	33	50

Table 41: 1989 Salary

Compensation Rank	Median	Middle 50% Range	
		Low	High
CEO	$713,000	$480,000	$750,000
Second highest	375,000	366,000	440,000
Third highest	306,000	300,000	350,000
Fourth highest	300,000	216,000	350,000
Fifth highest	277,000	215,000	325,000

Table 42: 1989 Salary Regression Formula

Compensation Rank	Formula	r^2
CEO	$\log Y = 2.1270 + 0.1860 \log X$	38%
Second highest	$\log Y = 2.1120 + 0.1360 \log X$	35
Third highest	$\log Y = 2.0550 + 0.1260 \log X$	26
Fourth highest	$\log Y = 1.9450 + 0.1420 \log X$	37
Fifth highest	$\log Y = 1.9040 + 0.1450 \log X$	40

Table 43: Salary as a Percentage of CEO's Salary

Compensation Rank	Median	Middle 50% Range	
		Low	High
Second highest	63%	52%	71%
Third highest	48	40	72
Fourth highest	45	40	57
Fifth highest	42	38	48

Consumer Chemicals

Chart 4: Total Current Compensation of the Five Highest-Paid Executives, by Company Sales

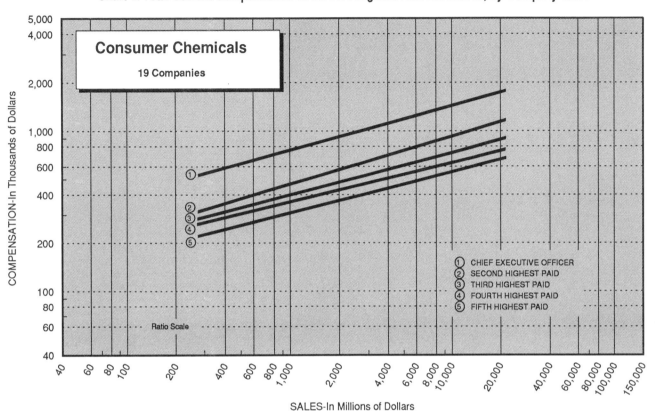

Consumer Chemicals

19 Companies

① CHIEF EXECUTIVE OFFICER
② SECOND HIGHEST PAID
③ THIRD HIGHEST PAID
④ FOURTH HIGHEST PAID
⑤ FIFTH HIGHEST PAID

COMPENSATION-In Thousands of Dollars

Ratio Scale

SALES-In Millions of Dollars

Table 44: 1989 Sales Volume

1989 Sales	Companies	
	Number	Percent
$5 billion and over	8	42%
2-4,999 billion	4	21
1-1,999 billion	1	5
500-999 million	3	16
300-499 million	2	11
200-299 million	1	5
Total	19	100%

	Middle 50% Range	
Median	Low	High
$4.2 billion	$930 million	$6.8 billion

Table 45: 1989 Total Current Compensation

Compensation Rank	Median	Middle 50% Range	
		Low	High
CEO	$1,150,000	$627,000	$1,505,000
Second highest	678,000	375,000	989,000
Third highest	568,000	327,000	736,000
Fourth highest	499,000	327,000	657,000
Fifth highest	430,000	260,000	540,000

Table 46: 1989 Total Current Compensation Regression Formula

Compensation Rank	Formula	r^2
CEO	log Y = 2.0600 + 0.2740 log X	46%
Second highest	log Y = 1.7830 + 0.2940 log X	56
Third highest	log Y = 1.8240 + 0.2600 log X	56
Fourth highest	log Y = 1.8320 + 0.2420 log X	56
Fifth highest	log Y = 1.7210 + 0.2570 log X	59

Table 47: Total Current Compensation as a Percentage of CEO's Total Current Compensation

Compensation Rank	Median	Middle 50% Range	
		Low	High
Second highest	59%	52%	81%
Third highest	52	45	65
Fourth highest	44	38	59
Fifth highest	37	34	49

Table 48: 1989 Salary

Compensation Rank	Median	Middle 50% Range	
		Low	High
CEO	$660,000	$441,000	$875,000
Second highest	348,000	280,000	504,000
Third highest	330,000	260,000	428,000
Fourth highest	320,000	238,000	405,000
Fifth highest	270,000	200,000	376,000

Table 49: 1989 Salary Regression Formula

Compensation Rank	Formula	r^2
CEO	log Y = 1.9800 + 0.2280 log X	54%
Second highest	log Y = 1.4640 + 0.3190 log X	76
Third highest	log Y = 1.5190 + 0.2830 log X	75
Fourth highest	log Y = 1.4870 + 0.2800 log X	75
Fifth highest	log Y = 1.4490 + 0.2760 log X	76

Table 50: Salary as a Percentage of CEO's Salary

Compensation Rank	Median	Middle 50% Range	
		Low	High
Second highest	64%	52%	79%
Third highest	51	47	64
Fourth highest	49	43	61
Fifth highest	41	39	57

Electrical and Electronic Machinery

Chart 5: Total Current Compensation of the Five Highest-Paid Executives, by Company Sales

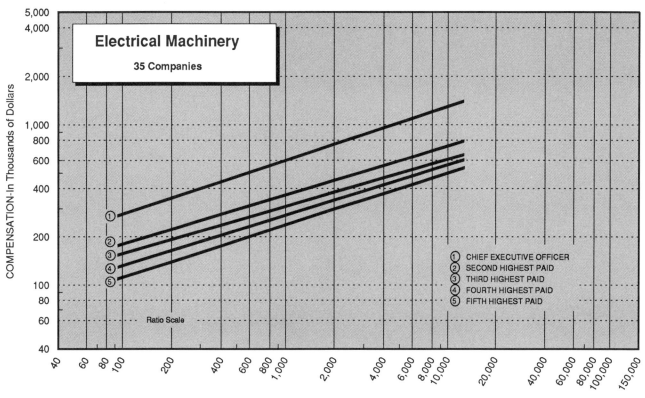

SALES-In Millions of Dollars

Table 51: 1989 Sales Volume

1989 Sales	Companies	
	Number	Percent
$5 billion and over	7	20%
2-4,999 billion	3	9
1-1,999 billion	3	9
500-999 million	9	26
300-499 million	4	11
200-299 million	6	17
199 million and under	3	9
Total	35	100%

Median	Middle 50% Range	
	Low	High
$631 million	$281 million	$3.1 billion

Table 52: 1989 Total Current Compensation

Compensation Rank	Median	Middle 50% Range	
		Low	High
CEO	$574,000	$408,000	$855,000
Second highest	340,000	242,000	460,000
Third highest	281,000	215,000	395,000
Fourth highest	258,000	185,000	382,000
Fifth highest	196,000	165,000	321,000

Table 53: 1989 Total Current Compensation Regression Formula

Compensation Rank	Formula	r^2
CEO	log Y = 1.7540 + 0.3410 log X	71%
Second highest	log Y = 1.6450 + 0.3060 log X	71
Third highest	log Y = 1.6000 + 0.2970 log X	78
Fourth highest	log Y = 1.4710 + 0.3210 log X	81
Fifth highest	log Y = 1.4230 + 0.3180 log X	75

Table 54: Total Current Compensation as a Percentage of CEO's Total Current Compensation

Compensation Rank	Median	Middle 50% Range	
		Low	High
Second highest	60%	49%	78%
Third highest	51	42	67
Fourth highest	43	39	50
Fifth highest	40	32	47

Table 55: 1989 Salary

Compensation Rank	Median	Middle 50% Range	
		Low	High
CEO	$375,000	$288,000	$602,000
Second highest	250,000	204,000	283,000
Third highest	216,000	158,000	250,000
Fourth highest	190,000	139,000	240,000
Fifth highest	153,000	134,000	225,000

Table 56: 1989 Salary Regression Formula

Compensation Rank	Formula	r^2
CEO	log Y = 1.8170 + 0.2520 log X	66%
Second highest	log Y = 1.8020 + 0.1950 log X	53
Third highest	log Y = 1.7580 + 0.1890 log X	51
Fourth highest	log Y = 1.6250 + 0.2150 log X	61
Fifth highest	log Y = 1.5820 + 0.2100 log X	38

Table 57: Salary as a Percentage of CEO's Salary

Compensation Rank	Median	Middle 50% Range	
		Low	High
Second highest	59%	52%	80%
Third highest	52	47	69
Fourth highest	45	42	62
Fifth highest	42	39	62

Fabricated Metal Products

Chart 6: Total Current Compensation of the Five Highest-Paid Executives, by Company Sales

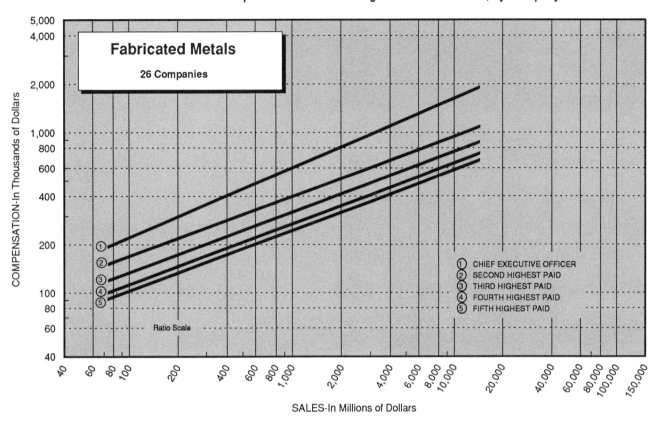

Fabricated Metals

26 Companies

COMPENSATION-In Thousands of Dollars

SALES-In Millions of Dollars

Ratio Scale

1. CHIEF EXECUTIVE OFFICER
2. SECOND HIGHEST PAID
3. THIRD HIGHEST PAID
4. FOURTH HIGHEST PAID
5. FIFTH HIGHEST PAID

Table 58: 1989 Sales Volume

1989 Sales	Companies Number	Percent
$5 billion and over	2	8%
2-4,999 billion	5	19
1-1,999 billion	4	15
500-999 million	4	15
300-499 million	6	23
200-299 million	3	12
199 million and under	2	8
Total	26	100%

Median	Middle 50% Range Low	High
$632 million	$361 million	$2.4 billion

Table 59: 1989 Total Current Compensation

Compensation Rank	Median	Middle 50% Range Low	High
CEO	$522,000	$346,000	$788,000
Second highest	351,000	245,000	586,000
Third highest	280,000	207,000	405,000
Fourth highest	232,000	189,000	337,000
Fifth highest	224,000	166,000	320,000

Table 60: 1989 Total Current Compensation Regression Formula

Compensation Rank	Formula	r^2
CEO	$\log Y = 1.4560 + 0.4400 \log X$	76%
Second highest	$\log Y = 1.4780 + 0.3740 \log X$	75
Third highest	$\log Y = 1.3660 + 0.3790 \log X$	78
Fourth highest	$\log Y = 1.2880 + 0.3800 \log X$	73
Fifth highest	$\log Y = 1.2600 + 0.3760 \log X$	76

Table 61: Total Current Compensation as a Percentage of CEO's Total Current Compensation

Compensation Rank	Median	Middle 50% Range	
		Low	High
Second highest	66%	61%	77%
Third highest	54	46	60
Fourth highest	44	41	55
Fifth highest	39	36	48

Table 62: 1989 Salary

Compensation Rank	Median	Middle 50% Range	
		Low	High
CEO	$385,000	$300,000	$525,000
Second highest	243,000	201,000	322,000
Third highest	205,000	155,000	250,000
Fourth highest	175,000	150,000	212,000
Fifth highest	163,000	135,000	196,000

Table 63: 1989 Salary Regression Formula

Compensation Rank	Formula	r^2
CEO	$\log Y = 1.6790 + 0.3020 \log X$	80%
Second highest	$\log Y = 1.7350 + 0.2270 \log X$	69
Third highest	$\log Y = 1.5870 + 0.2460 \log X$	67
Fourth highest	$\log Y = 1.5450 + 0.2400 \log X$	76
Fifth highest	$\log Y = 1.4870 + 0.2480 \log X$	75

Table 64: Salary as a Percentage of CEO's Salary

Compensation Rank	Median	Middle 50% Range	
		Low	High
Second highest	71%	63%	76%
Third highest	55	48	63
Fourth highest	48	44	54
Fifth highest	44	39	49

Food and Kindred Products

Chart 7: Total Current Compensation of the Five Highest-Paid Executives, by Company Sales

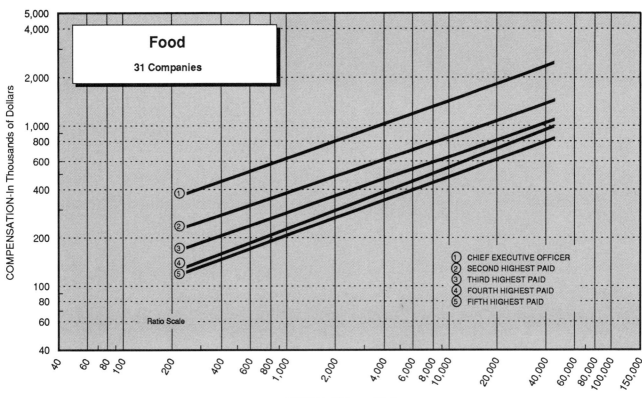

SALES-In Millions of Dollars

Table 65: 1989 Sales Volume

	Companies	
1989 Sales	Number	Percent
$5 billion and over	12	39%
2-4,999 billion	5	16
1-1,999 billion	6	19
500-999 million	5	16
300-499 million	1	3
200-299 million	2	7
Total	31	100%

	Middle 50% Range	
Median	Low	High
$2.4 billion	$993 million	$7.9 billion

Table 66: 1989 Total Current Compensation

		Middle 50% Range	
Compensation Rank	Median	Low	High
CEO	$1,040,000	$677,000	$1,464,000
Second highest	582,000	385,000	885,000
Third highest	448,000	285,000	642,000
Fourth highest	396,000	208,000	525,000
Fifth highest	346,000	245,000	507,000

Table 67: 1989 Total Current Compensation Regression Formula

Compensation Rank	Formula	r^2
CEO	log Y = 1.7260 + 0.3570 log X	50%
Second highest	log Y = 1.5610 + 0.3400 log X	44
Third highest	log Y = 1.4090 + 0.3480 log X	55
Fourth highest	log Y = 1.1620 + 0.3960 log X	62
Fifth highest	log Y = 1.2300 + 0.3640 log X	64

Table 68: Total Current Compensation as a Percentage of CEO's Total Current Compensation

Compensation Rank	Median	Middle 50% Range	
		Low	High
Second highest	61%	51%	73%
Third highest	42	38	52
Fourth highest	37	34	42
Fifth highest	32	28	38

Table 69: 1989 Salary

Compensation Rank	Median	Middle 50% Range	
		Low	High
CEO	$500,000	$300,000	$787,000
Second highest	363,000	225,000	490,000
Third highest	291,000	198,000	363,000
Fourth highest	244,000	155,000	300,000
Fifth highest	191,000	125,000	310,000

Table 70: 1989 Salary Regression Formula

Compensation Rank	Formula	r^2
CEO	log Y = 1.7440 + 0.2770 log X	52%
Second highest	log Y = 1.5090 + 0.2970 log X	54
Third highest	log Y = 1.3990 + 0.2990 log X	67
Fourth highest	log Y = 1.1580 + 0.3450 log X	68
Fifth highest	log Y = 1.0210 + 0.3670 log X	75

Table 71: Salary as a Percentage of CEO's Salary

Compensation Rank	Median	Middle 50% Range	
		Low	High
Second highest	67%	61%	74%
Third highest	52	45	62
Fourth highest	44	38	52
Fifth highest	39	32	47

Industrial Chemicals

Chart 8: Total Current Compensation of the Five Highest-Paid Executives, by Company Sales

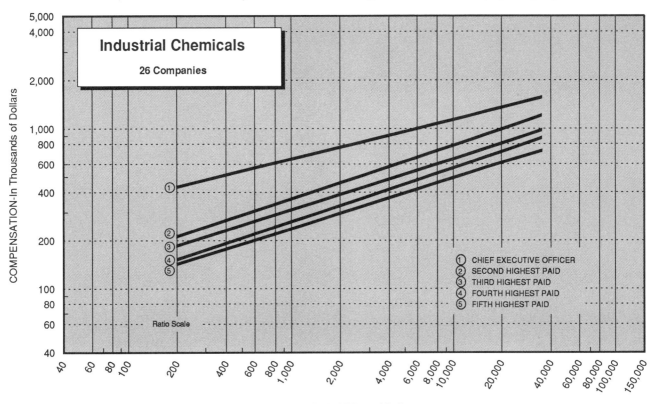

SALES-In Millions of Dollars

Table 72: 1989 Sales Volume

	Companies	
1989 Sales	Number	Percent
$5 billion and over	5	19%
2-4,999 billion	5	19
1-1,999 billion	6	23
500-999 million	6	23
300-499 million	3	12
200-299 million	1	4
Total	26	100%

	Middle 50% Range	
Median	Low	High
$1.4 billion	$658 million	$2.7 billion

Table 73: 1989 Total Current Compensation

		Middle 50% Range	
Compensation Rank	Median	Low	High
CEO	$722,000	$547,000	$1,042,000
Second highest	428,000	290,000	623,000
Third highest	352,000	270,000	527,000
Fourth highest	293,000	231,000	453,000
Fifth highest	259,000	224,000	350,000

Table 74: 1989 Total Current Compensation Regression Formula

Compensation Rank	Formula	r^2
CEO	log Y = 2.0700 + 0.2470 log X	59%
Second highest	log Y = 1.5710 + 0.3300 log X	80
Third highest	log Y = 1.5290 + 0.3210 log X	80
Fourth highest	log Y = 1.4150 + 0.3360 log X	83
Fifth highest	log Y = 1.4390 + 0.3130 log X	77

Table 75: Total Current Compensation as a Percentage of CEO's Total Current Compensation

Compensation Rank	Median	Middle 50% Range	
		Low	High
Second highest	66%	48%	70%
Third highest	52	44	59
Fourth highest	44	39	50
Fifth highest	40	32	45

Table 76: 1989 Salary

Compensation Rank	Median	Middle 50% Range	
		Low	High
CEO	$465,000	$375,000	$584,000
Second highest	325,000	210,000	389,000
Third highest	245,000	187,000	369,000
Fourth highest	228,000	169,000	263,000
Fifth highest	200,000	165,000	254,000

Table 77: 1989 Salary Regression Formula

Compensation Rank	Formula	r^2
CEO	log Y = 1.9300 + 0.2250 log X	49%
Second highest	log Y = 1.7200 + 0.2310 log X	55
Third highest	log Y = 1.6630 + 0.2200 log X	54
Fourth highest	log Y = 1.5660 + 0.2350 log X	60
Fifth highest	log Y = 1.5630 + 0.2230 log X	57

Table 78: Salary as a Percentage of CEO's Salary

Compensation Rank	Median	Middle 50% Range	
		Low	High
Second highest	66%	57%	75%
Third highest	53	46	62
Fourth highest	45	44	57
Fifth highest	43	36	46

Machinery (except Electrical)

Chart 9: Total Current Compensation of the Five Highest-Paid Executives, by Company Sales

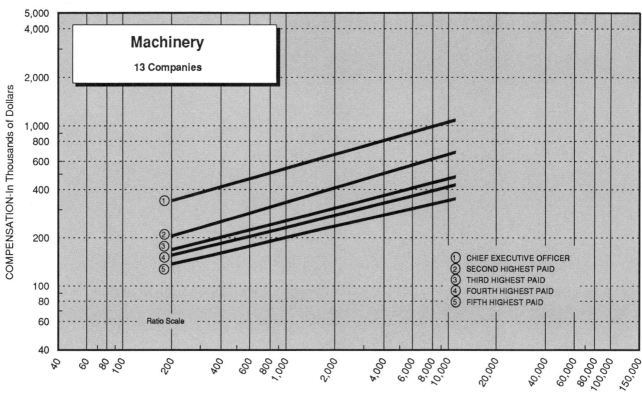

SALES-In Millions of Dollars

Table 79: 1989 Sales Volume

1989 Sales	Companies	
	Number	Percent
$5 billion and over	3	23%
2-4,999 billion	2	15
1-1,999 billion	2	15
500-999 million	3	23
300-499 million	—	—
200-299 million	3	23
199 million and under	—	—
Total	13	100%

	Middle 50% Range	
Median	Low	High
$1.9 billion	$526 million	$3.2 billion

Table 80: 1989 Total Current Compensation

Compensation Rank	Median	Middle 50% Range	
		Low	High
CEO	$658,000	$424,000	$889,000
Second highest	334,000	267,000	553,000
Third highest	251,000	229,000	382,000
Fourth highest	250,000	198,000	342,000
Fifth highest	211,000	155,000	275,000

Table 81: 1989 Total Current Compensation Regression Formula

Compensation Rank	Formula	r^2
CEO	log Y = 1.8560 + 0.2930 log X	55%
Second highest	log Y = 1.6150 + 0.3030 log X	57
Third highest	log Y = 1.6220 + 0.2630 log X	78
Fourth highest	log Y = 1.6170 + 0.2510 log X	85
Fifth highest	log Y = 1.6240 + 0.2280 log X	67

Table 82: Total Current Compensation as a Percentage of CEO's Total Current Compensation

Compensation Rank	Median	Middle 50% Range	
		Low	High
Second highest	63%	55%	73%
Third highest	50	37	54
Fourth highest	43	34	54
Fifth highest	34	27	52

Table 83: 1989 Salary

Compensation Rank	Median	Middle 50% Range	
		Low	High
CEO	$403,000	$275,000	$581,000
Second highest	230,000	150,000	334,000
Third highest	162,000	147,000	292,000
Fourth highest	162,000	132,000	259,000
Fifth highest	155,000	127,000	211,000

Table 84: 1989 Salary Regression Formula

Compensation Rank	Formula	r^2
CEO	log Y = 1.9520 + 0.2000 log X	38%
Second highest	log Y = 1.7270 + 0.2030 log X	47
Third highest	log Y = 1.6620 + 0.1980 log X	60
Fourth highest	log Y = 1.6130 + 0.2040 log X	65
Fifth highest	log Y = 1.6300 + 0.1870 log X	59

Table 85: Salary as a Percentage of CEO's Salary

Compensation Rank	Median	Middle 50% Range	
		Low	High
Second highest	60%	51%	73%
Third highest	50	38	58
Fourth highest	46	36	57
Fifth highest	42	36	55

Paper

Chart 10: Total Current Compensation of the Five Highest-Paid Executives, by Company Sales

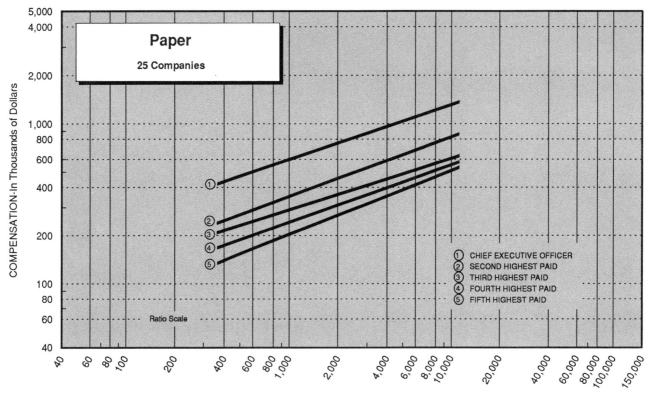

SALES-In Millions of Dollars

Table 86: 1989 Sales Volume

	Companies	
1989 Sales	Number	Percent
$5 billion and over	7	28%
2-4,999 billion	5	20
1-1,999 billion	5	20
500-999 million.............................	6	24
499 million and under.......................	2	8
Total	25	100%

	Middle 50% Range	
Median	Low	High
$1.9 billion	$849 million	$5.1 billion

Table 87: 1989 Total Current Compensation

		Middle 50% Range	
Compensation Rank	Median	Low	High
CEO	$819,000	$526,000	$1,082,000
Second highest	532,000	302,000	633,000
Third highest	382,000	289,000	497,000
Fourth highest	310,000	241,000	450,000
Fifth highest	266,000	213,000	372,000

Table 88: 1989 Total Current Compensation Regression Formula

Compensation Rank	Formula	r^2
CEO	log Y = 1.7610 + 0.3390 log X	49%
Second highest	log Y = 1.4380 + 0.3700 log X	50
Third highest	log Y = 1.5060 + 0.3180 log X	46
Fourth highest	log Y = 1.2970 + 0.3620 log X	62
Fifth highest	log Y = 1.1270 + 0.3940 log X	74

Table 89: Total Current Compensation as a Percentage of CEO's Total Current Compensation

Compensation Rank	Median	Middle 50% Range	
		Low	High
Second highest	61%	56%	68%
Third highest	48	42	54
Fourth highest	42	36	47
Fifth highest	39	33	43

Table 90: 1989 Salary

Compensation Rank	Median	Middle 50% Range	
		Low	High
CEO	$508,000	$390,000	$636,000
Second highest	300,000	245,000	391,000
Third highest	260,000	203,000	307,000
Fourth highest	241,000	180,000	266,000
Fifth highest	210,000	165,000	250,000

Table 91: 1989 Salary Regression Formula

Compensation Rank	Formula	r^2
CEO	log Y = 1.6110 + 0.3310 log X	72%
Second highest	log Y = 1.3770 + 0.3320 log X	64
Third highest	log Y = 1.5280 + 0.2590 log X	51
Fourth highest	log Y = 1.3770 + 0.2880 log X	65
Fifth highest	log Y = 1.3850 + 0.2750 log X	61

Table 92: Salary as a Percentage of CEO's Salary

Compensation Rank	Median	Middle 50% Range	
		Low	High
Second highest	59%	56%	67%
Third highest	47	41	55
Fourth highest	41	38	49
Fifth highest	41	33	43

Plastic, Rubber, and Leather Products

Chart 11: Total Current Compensation of the Five Highest-Paid Executives, by Company Sales

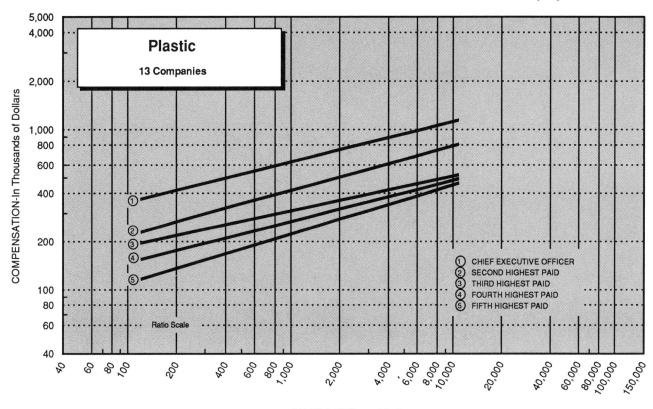

Table 93: 1989 Sales Volume

1989 Sales	Companies	
	Number	Percent
$5 billion and over	1	8%
2-4,999 billion	1	8
1-1,999 billion	3	23
500-999 million	3	23
300-499 million	1	8
200-299 million	2	15
199 million and under	2	15
Total	13	100%

Median	Middle 50% Range	
	Low	High
$543 million	$278 million	$1.3 billion

Table 94: 1989 Total Current Compensation

Compensation Rank	Median	Middle 50% Range	
		Low	High
CEO	$583,000	$373,000	$889,000
Second highest	359,000	283,000	531,000
Third highest	274,000	245,000	340,000
Fourth highest	235,000	185,000	315,000
Fifth highest	215,000	134,000	262,000

Table 95: 1989 Total Current Compensation Regression Formula

Compensation Rank	Formula	r^2
CEO	log Y = 2.0460 + 0.2500 log X	41%
Second highest	log Y = 1.7980 + 0.2760 log X	61
Third highest	log Y = 1.9420 + 0.1820 log X	57
Fourth highest	log Y = 1.5540 + 0.2910 log X	75
Fifth highest	log Y = 1.3940 + 0.3200 log X	78

Table 96: Total Current Compensation as a Percentage of CEO's Total Current Compensation

| Compensation Rank | Median | Middle 50% Range | |
		Low	High
Second highest	77%	57%	83%
Third highest	50	45	65
Fourth highest	45	38	56
Fifth highest	39	27	45

Table 97: 1989 Salary

| Compensation Rank | Median | Middle 50% Range | |
		Low	High
CEO	$324,000	$257,000	$600,000
Second highest	195,000	179,000	264,000
Third highest	176,000	142,000	250,000
Fourth highest	140,000	100,000	166,000
Fifth highest	134,000	105,000	152,000

Table 98: 1989 Salary Regression Formula

Compensation Rank	Formula	r^2
CEO	log Y = 2.1130 + 0.1720 log X	23%
Second highest	log Y = 1.6530 + 0.2530 log X	57
Third highest	log Y = 1.7410 + 0.1800 log X	35
Fourth highest	log Y = 1.4810 + 0.2460 log X	61
Fifth highest	log Y = 1.5150 + 0.2290 log X	78

Table 99: Salary as a Percentage of CEO's Salary

| Compensation Rank | Median | Middle 50% Range | |
		Low	High
Second highest	63%	50%	79%
Third highest	48	30	62
Fourth highest	41	30	54
Fifth highest	40	27	52

Primary Metals (including Steel)

Chart 12: Total Current Compensation of the Five Highest-Paid Executives, by Company Sales

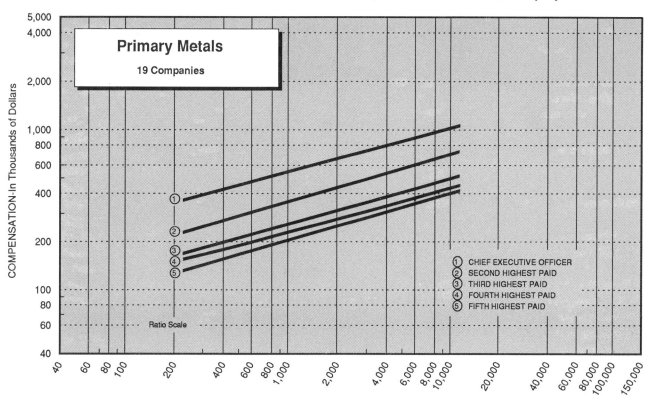

Primary Metals

19 Companies

COMPENSATION-In Thousands of Dollars

Ratio Scale

① CHIEF EXECUTIVE OFFICER
② SECOND HIGHEST PAID
③ THIRD HIGHEST PAID
④ FOURTH HIGHEST PAID
⑤ FIFTH HIGHEST PAID

SALES-In Millions of Dollars

Table 100: 1989 Sales Volume

1989 Sales	Companies	
	Number	Percent
$5 billion and over	2	11%
2-4,999 billion	5	26
1-1,999 billion	3	16
500-999 million	2	11
300-499 million	5	26
200-299 million	2	11
199 million and under	—	—
Total	19	100%

Median	Middle 50% Range	
	Low	High
$1.3 billion	$373 million	$2.6 billion

Table 101: 1989 Total Current Compensation

Compensation Rank	Median	Middle 50% Range	
		Low	High
CEO	$600,000	$396,000	$740,000
Second highest	327,000	246,000	521,000
Third highest	243,000	180,000	399,000
Fourth highest	212,000	168,000	350,000
Fifth highest	187,000	155,000	327,000

Table 102: 1989 Total Current Compensation Regression Formula

Compensation Rank	Formula	r^2
CEO	log Y = 1.9210 + 0.2720 log X	45%
Second highest	log Y = 1.6490 + 0.3010 log X	50
Third highest	log Y = 1.5450 + 0.2880 log X	58
Fourth highest	log Y = 1.5200 + 0.2790 log X	51
Fifth highest	log Y = 1.3690 + 0.3160 log X	62

Table 103: Total Current Compensation as a Percentage of CEO's Total Current Compensation

Compensation Rank	Median	Middle 50% Range	
		Low	High
Second highest	68%	59%	76%
Third highest	51	38	61
Fourth highest	40	37	52
Fifth highest	38	33	47

Table 104: 1989 Salary

Compensation Rank	Median	Middle 50% Range	
		Low	High
CEO	$425,000	$270,000	$540,000
Second highest	246,000	173,000	360,000
Third highest	210,000	150,000	273,000
Fourth highest	168,000	139,000	240,000
Fifth highest		Insufficient data	

Table 105: 1989 Salary Regression Formula

Compensation Rank	Formula	r^2
CEO	log Y = 1.8870 + 0.2270 log X	42%
Second highest	log Y = 1.5060 + 0.2930 log X	46
Third highest	log Y = 1.3980 + 0.2880 log X	52
Fourth highest	log Y = 1.3980 + 0.2740 log X	50
Fifth highest	log Y = 1.2740 + 0.3040 log X	67

Table 106: Salary as a Percentage of CEO's Salary

Compensation Rank	Median	Middle 50% Range	
		Low	High
Second highest	67%	56%	75%
Third highest	52	43	58
Fourth highest	47	40	52
Fifth highest	48	39	51

Transportation Equipment

Chart 13: Total Current Compensation of the Five Highest-Paid Executives, by Company Sales

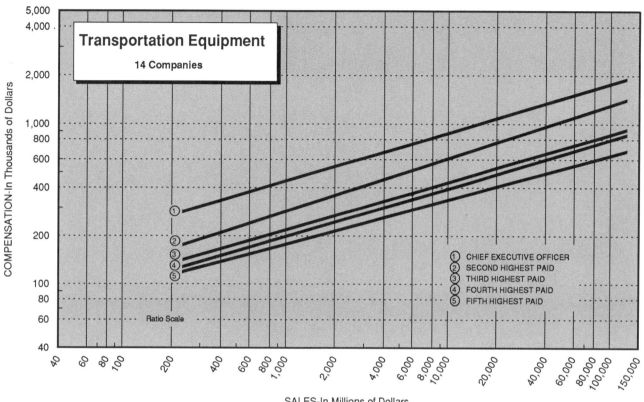

SALES-In Millions of Dollars

Table 107: 1989 Sales Volume

1989 Sales	Companies	
	Number	Percent
$5 billion and over	3	21%
2-4,999 billion	5	36
1-1,999 billion	1	7
500-999 million	1	7
300-499 million	2	14
200-299 million	2	14
Total	14	100%

	Middle 50% Range	
Median	Low	High
$3.3 billion	$438 million	$4.9 billion

Table 108: 1989 Total Current Compensation

Compensation Rank	Median	Middle 50% Range	
		Low	High
CEO	$452,000	$418,000	$1,060,000
Second highest	371,000	177,000	606,000
Third highest	250,000	169,000	440,000
Fourth highest	235,000	144,000	378,000
Fifth highest	220,000	135,000	361,000

Table 109: 1989 Total Current Compensation Regression Formula

Compensation Rank	Formula	r^2
CEO	log Y = 1.7490 + 0.2980 log X	74%
Second highest	log Y = 1.4910 + 0.3220 log X	80
Third highest	log Y = 1.4760 + 0.2870 log X	82
Fourth highest	log Y = 1.4180 + 0.2950 log X	85
Fifth highest	log Y = 1.4120 + 0.2790 log X	71

Table 110: Total Current Compensation as a Percentage of CEO's Total Current Compensation

Compensation Rank	Median	Middle 50% Range	
		Low	High
Second highest	67%	57%	81%
Third highest	47	44	56
Fourth highest	45	38	52
Fifth highest	39	34	45

Table 111: 1989 Salary

Compensation Rank	Median	Middle 50% Range	
		Low	High
CEO	$450,000	$271,000	$650,000
Second highest	371,000	164,000	435,000
Third highest	250,000	152,000	310,000
Fourth highest	243,000	135,000	328,000
Fifth highest	220,000	118,000	270,000

Table 112: 1989 Salary Regression Formula

Compensation Rank	Formula	r^2
CEO	log Y = 1.6970 + 0.2730 log X	86%
Second highest	log Y = 1.4560 + 0.2940 log X	89
Third highest	log Y = 1.4980 + 0.2490 log X	86
Fourth highest	log Y = 1.4620 + 0.2540 log X	93
Fifth highest	log Y = 1.4760 + 0.2310 log X	90

Table 113: Salary as a Percentage of CEO's Salary

Compensation Rank	Median	Middle 50% Range	
		Low	High
Second highest	69%	57%	82%
Third highest	52	47	56
Fourth highest	51	42	55
Fifth highest	44	36	47

Commercial Banking

Chart 14: Total Current Compensation of the Five Highest-Paid Executives, by Total Assets

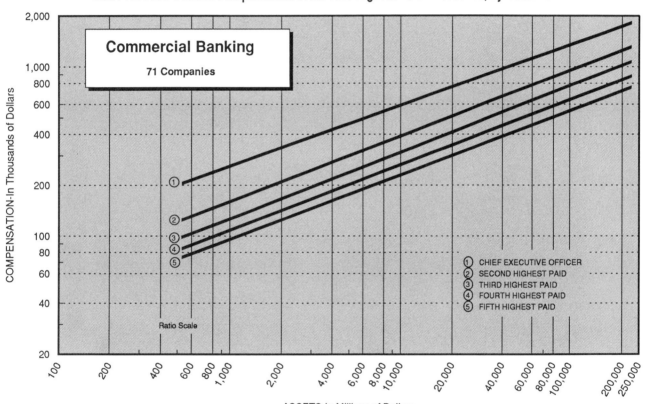

Table 114: 1989 Total Assets

1989 Total Assets	Companies	
	Number	Percent
$5 billion and over	40	56%
2-4,999 billion	16	23
1-1,999 billion	9	13
500-999 million	6	9
Total	71	100%

Median	Middle 50% Range	
	Low	High
$6.0 billion	$2.4 billion	$12.3 billion

Table 115: 1989 Total Current Compensation

Compensation Rank	Median	Middle 50% Range	
		Low	High
CEO	$479,000	$329,000	$710,000
Second highest	333,000	201,000	465,000
Third highest	270,000	166,000	369,000
Fourth highest	211,000	140,000	332,000
Fifth highest	188,000	124,000	275,000

Table 116: 1989 Total Current Compensation Regression Formula

Compensation Rank	Formula	r^2
CEO	$\log Y = 1.3230 + 0.3620 \log X$	69%
Second highest	$\log Y = 1.0520 + 0.3830 \log X$	66
Third highest	$\log Y = 0.9360 + 0.3900 \log X$	70
Fourth highest	$\log Y = 0.8650 + 0.3890 \log X$	73
Fifth highest	$\log Y = 0.8280 + 0.3840 \log X$	69

Table 117: Total Current Compensation as a Percentage of CEO's Total Current Compensation

Compensation Rank	Median	Middle 50% Range	
		Low	High
Second highest	64%	57%	73%
Third highest	53	45	61
Fourth highest	44	38	50
Fifth highest	40	33	46

Table 118: 1989 Salary

Compensation Rank	Median	Middle 50% Range	
		Low	High
CEO	$375,000	$275,000	$495,000
Second highest	258,000	170,000	332,000
Third highest	218,000	145,000	270,000
Fourth highest	175,000	121,000	240,000
Fifth highest	153,000	115,000	200,000

Table 119: 1989 Salary Regression Formula

Compensation Rank	Formula	r^2
CEO	$\log Y = 1.5080 + 0.2800 \log X$	66%
Second highest	$\log Y = 1.2720 + 0.2950 \log X$	63
Third highest	$\log Y = 1.1310 + 0.3110 \log X$	67
Fourth highest	$\log Y = 1.0630 + 0.3110 \log X$	75
Fifth highest	$\log Y = 1.0990 + 0.2850 \log X$	47

Table 120: Salary as a Percentage of CEO's Salary

Compensation Rank	Median	Middle 50% Range	
		Low	High
Second highest	66%	59%	72%
Third highest	55	47	63
Fourth highest	46	40	54
Fifth highest	42	35	50

Table 121: 1989 Bonus Awards (as Percent of Salary), by Company Size

	Total Assets		
	Middle 50% Range		
	Low	Median	High
	$2.4	$6.0	$12.3
Executive	Billion	Billion	Billion
CEO			
1989 Bonus	35%	41%	46%
Salary	$283,000	$365,000	$446,000
Second Highest			
1989 Bonus	29%	37%	44%
Salary	$188,000	$242,000	$296,000
Third Highest			
1989 Bonus	26%	33%	39%
Salary	$151,000	$200,000	$250,000
Fourth Highest			
1989 Bonus	24%	31%	37%
Salary	$127,000	$170,000	$212,000
Fifth Highest			
1989 Bonus	21%	31%	40%
Salary	$113,000	$147,000	$181,000

Table 122: 1989 Bonus Awards

1989 Bonus Awards (Percent of Salary)	CEOS Number	CEOS Percent	Second Highest Paid Number	Second Highest Paid Percent	Third Highest Paid Number	Third Highest Paid Percent	Fourth Highest Paid Number	Fourth Highest Paid Percent	Fifth Highest Paid Number	Fifth Highest Paid Percent
100% or more	4	7%	4	7%	3	6%	3	6%	2	4%
70-99	6	11	5	9	6	12	5	10	3	6
60-69	1	2	1	2	1	2	2	4	3	6
50-59	8	15	7	13	3	6	1	2	4	8
40-49	11	20	8	15	11	22	9	17	5	10
30-39	9	17	8	15	9	18	6	12	14	27
20-29	7	13	7	13	5	10	8	15	5	10
Less than 20%	8	15	15	27	12	24	18	35	16	31
Total	54	100%	55	100%	50	100%	52	100%	52	100%
Median Bonus	40%		37%		38%		29%		35%	
Middle 50% Range	27 – 52%		19 – 52%		21 – 53%		15 – 43%		16 – 45%	

Communications

Chart 15: Total Current Compensation of the Five Highest-Paid Executives, by Company Sales

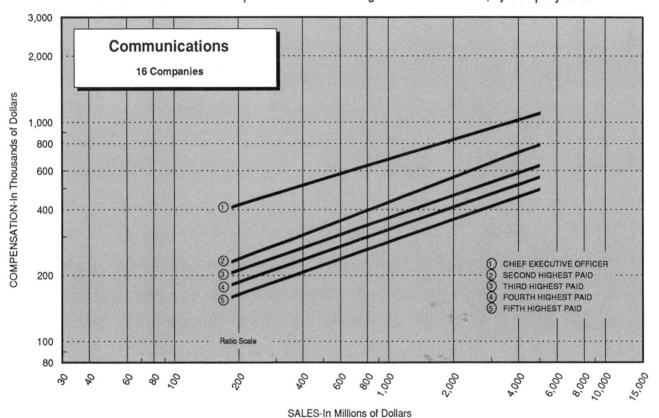

Table 123: 1989 Sales Volume

	Companies	
1989 Sales	Number	Percent
$2 billion and over	6	38%
1-1,999 billion	4	25
500-999 million	1	6
300-499 million	4	25
200-299 million	—	—
199 million and under	1	6
Total	16	100%

	Middle 50% Range	
Median	Low	High
$1.3 billion	$463 million	$2.5 billion

Table 124: 1989 Total Current Compensation

		Middle 50% Range	
Compensation Rank	Median	Low	High
CEO	$629,000	$568,000	$920,000
Second highest	472,000	341,000	637,000
Third highest	392,000	262,000	522,000
Fourth highest	371,000	256,000	494,000
Fifth highest	297,000	240,000	400,000

Table 125: 1989 Total Current Compensation Regression Formula

Compensation Rank	Formula	r^2
CEO	$\log Y = 1.9480 + 0.2950 \log X$	55%
Second highest	$\log Y = 1.5220 + 0.3720 \log X$	58
Third highest	$\log Y = 1.5480 + 0.3380 \log X$	51
Fourth highest	$\log Y = 1.4860 + 0.3420 \log X$	52
Fifth highest	$\log Y = 1.4180 + 0.3450 \log X$	63

Table 126: Total Current Compensation as a Percentage of CEO's Total Current Compensation

Compensation Rank	Median	Middle 50% Range Low	High
Second highest	66%	51%	80%
Third highest	51	44	60
Fourth highest	44	42	53
Fifth highest	40	34	50

Table 127: 1989 Salary

Compensation Rank	Median	Middle 50% Range Low	High
CEO	$525,000	$450,000	$629,000
Second highest	350,000	324,000	382,000
Third highest	306,000	267,000	382,000
Fourth highest	267,000	263,000	356,000
Fifth highest	254,000	209,000	316,000

Table 128: 1989 Salary Regression Formula

Compensation Rank	Formula	r^2
CEO	$\log Y = 2.2980 + 0.1380 \log X$	25%
Second highest	$\log Y = 1.7820 + 0.2370 \log X$	62
Third highest	$\log Y = 1.8250 + 0.2090 \log X$	45
Fourth highest	$\log Y = 1.8660 + 0.1860 \log X$	47
Fifth highest	$\log Y = 1.4130 + 0.3120 \log X$	79

Table 129: Salary as a Percentage of CEO's Salary

Compensation Rank	Median	Middle 50% Range Low	High
Second highest	62%	54%	76%
Third highest	53	46	68
Fourth highest	50	44	60
Fifth highest	41	38	53

Table 130: 1989 Bonus Awards (as Percent of Salary), by Company Size

Executive	Sales Volume — Middle 50% Range		
	Low $463 Million	Median $1.3 Billion	High $2.5 Billion
CEO			
1989 Bonus	39%	48%	54%
Salary	$465,000	$532,000	$580,000
Second Highest			
1989 Bonus	34%	43%	49%
Salary	$257,000	$339,000	$404,000
Third Highest			
1989 Bonus	31%	41%	48%
Salary	$239,000	$303,000	$351,000
Fourth Highest			
1989 Bonus	31%	40%	46%
Salary	$226,000	$284,000	$328,000
Fifth Highest			
1989 Bonus	23%	35%	44%
Salary	$173,000	$249,000	$313,000

Diversified Service

Chart 16: Total Current Compensation of the Five Highest-Paid Executives, by Company Sales

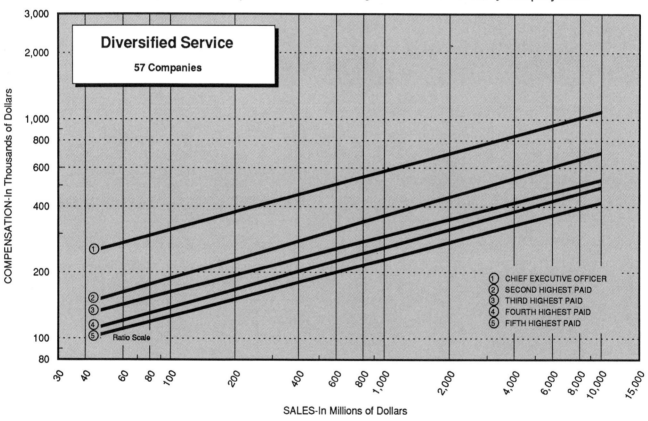

Diversified Service

57 Companies

COMPENSATION-In Thousands of Dollars

① CHIEF EXECUTIVE OFFICER
② SECOND HIGHEST PAID
③ THIRD HIGHEST PAID
④ FOURTH HIGHEST PAID
⑤ FIFTH HIGHEST PAID

Ratio Scale

SALES-In Millions of Dollars

Table 131: 1989 Sales Volume

1989 Sales	Companies Number	Companies Percent
$5 billion and over	6	11%
2-4,999 billion	8	14
1-1,999 billion	7	12
500-999 million	13	23
300-499 million	7	12
200-299 million	9	16
199 million and under	7	12
Total	57	100%

Median	Middle 50% Range Low	Middle 50% Range High
$702 million	$288 million	$1.8 billion

Table 132: 1989 Total Current Compensation

Compensation Rank	Median	Middle 50% Range Low	Middle 50% Range High
CEO	$510,000	$351,000	$817,000
Second highest	352,000	228,000	441,000
Third highest	272,000	182,000	380,000
Fourth highest	240,000	175,000	331,000
Fifth highest	190,000	156,000	289,000

Table 133: 1989 Total Current Compensation Regression Formula

Compensation Rank	Formula	r^2
CEO	$\log Y = 1.9610 + 0.2670 \log X$	33%
Second highest	$\log Y = 1.7180 + 0.2820 \log X$	52
Third highest	$\log Y = 1.7010 + 0.2550 \log X$	45
Fourth highest	$\log Y = 1.5980 + 0.2720 \log X$	51
Fifth highest	$\log Y = 1.5580 + 0.2650 \log X$	50

Table 134: Total Current Compensation as a Percentage of CEO's Total Current Compensation

Compensation Rank	Median	Middle 50% Range Low	Middle 50% Range High
Second highest	70%	55%	79%
Third highest	52	43	65
Fourth highest	49	39	57
Fifth highest	42	36	51

Table 135: 1989 Salary

Compensation Rank	Median	Middle 50% Range Low	Middle 50% Range High
CEO	$375,000	$258,000	$575,000
Second highest	245,000	175,000	332,000
Third highest	195,000	145,000	276,000
Fourth highest	175,000	129,000	240,000
Fifth highest	148,000	115,000	236,000

Table 136: 1989 Salary Regression Formula

Compensation Rank	Formula	r^2
CEO	$\log Y = 1.9690 + 0.2120 \log X$	25%
Second highest	$\log Y = 1.7120 + 0.2330 \log X$	50
Third highest	$\log Y = 1.7010 + 0.2060 \log X$	51
Fourth highest	$\log Y = 1.5910 + 0.2290 \log X$	51
Fifth highest	$\log Y = 1.5580 + 0.2250 \log X$	49

Table 137: Salary as a Percentage of CEO's Salary

Compensation Rank	Median	Middle 50% Range Low	Middle 50% Range High
Second highest	67%	54%	81%
Third highest	55	45	63
Fourth highest	50	40	60
Fifth highest	46	36	57

Table 138: 1989 Bonus Awards (as Percent of Salary), by Company Size

Executive	Sales Volume Low $288 Million	Sales Volume Median $702 Million	Sales Volume High $1.8 Billion
CEO			
1989 Bonus	40%	47%	54%
Salary	$317,000	$382,000	$465,000
Second Highest			
1989 Bonus	38%	45%	52%
Salary	$197,000	$243,000	$304,000
Third Highest			
1989 Bonus	36%	43%	50%
Salary	$165,000	$198,000	$241,000
Fourth Highest			
1989 Bonus	34%	40%	46%
Salary	$145,000	$178,000	$221,000
Fifth Highest			
1989 Bonus	31%	35%	40%
Salary	$131,000	$160,000	$198,000

Table 139: 1989 Bonus Awards

1989 Bonus Awards (Percent of Salary)	CEOS Number	CEOS Percent	Second Highest Paid Number	Second Highest Paid Percent	Third Highest Paid Number	Third Highest Paid Percent	Fourth Highest Paid Number	Fourth Highest Paid Percent	Fifth Highest Paid Number	Fifth Highest Paid Percent
100% or more	5	12%	4	9%	2	4%	2	5%	—	—
70-99	9	21	8	19	5	11	4	10	5	11%
60-69	7	16	5	12	4	9	5	12	3	7
50-59	3	7	8	19	9	20	11	26	6	14
40-49	6	14	4	9	8	18	8	19	10	23
30-39	2	5	5	12	8	18	4	10	7	16
20-29	4	9	5	12	4	9	4	10	3	7
Less than 20%	7	16	4	9	5	11	4	10	10	23
Total	43	100%	43	100%	45	100%	42	100%	44	100%
Median Bonus	55%		50%		48%		50%		44%	
Middle 50% Range	24 – 76%		35 – 71%		34 – 58%		34 – 60%		20 – 50%	

Energy and Natural Resources

Chart 17: Total Current Compensation of the Five Highest-Paid Executives, by Company Sales

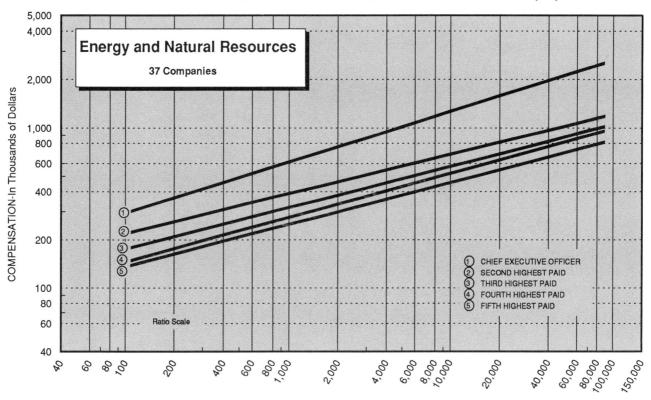

Energy and Natural Resources

37 Companies

COMPENSATION-In Thousands of Dollars

SALES-In Millions of Dollars

Ratio Scale

① CHIEF EXECUTIVE OFFICER
② SECOND HIGHEST PAID
③ THIRD HIGHEST PAID
④ FOURTH HIGHEST PAID
⑤ FIFTH HIGHEST PAID

Table 140: 1989 Sales Volume

1989 Sales	Companies	
	Number	Percent
$5 billion and over	11	30%
2-4,999 billion	4	11
1-1,999 billion	8	22
500-999 million	7	19
300-499 million	2	5
200-299 million	—	—
199 million and under	5	14
Total	37	100%

Median	Middle 50% Range	
	Low	High
$1.7 billion	$659 million	$9.8 billion

Table 141: 1989 Total Current Compensation

Compensation Rank	Median	Middle 50% Range	
		Low	High
CEO	$680,000	$440,000	$1,050,000
Second highest	420,000	294,000	693,000
Third highest	350,000	229,000	483,000
Fourth highest	254,000	185,000	440,000
Fifth highest	223,000	169,000	381,000

Table 142: 1989 Total Current Compensation Regression Formula

Compensation Rank	Formula	r^2
CEO	$\log Y = 1.8410 + 0.3150 \log X$	63%
Second highest	$\log Y = 1.8570 + 0.2460 \log X$	64
Third highest	$\log Y = 1.7300 + 0.2580 \log X$	74
Fourth highest	$\log Y = 1.6130 + 0.2760 \log X$	75
Fifth highest	$\log Y = 1.6000 + 0.2660 \log X$	69

Table 143: Total Current Compensation as a Percentage of CEO's Total Current Compensation

Compensation Rank	Median	Middle 50% Range	
		Low	High
Second highest	67%	55%	79%
Third highest	50	40	60
Fourth highest	41	36	51
Fifth highest	38	32	48

Table 144: 1989 Salary

Compensation Rank	Median	Middle 50% Range	
		Low	High
CEO	$460,000	$350,000	$585,000
Second highest	312,000	264,000	429,000
Third highest	257,000	203,000	317,000
Fourth highest	200,000	161,000	300,000
Fifth highest	180,000	158,000	240,000

Table 145: 1989 Salary Regression Formula

Compensation Rank	Formula	r^2
CEO	$\log Y = 2.0520 + 0.1830 \log X$	73%
Second highest	$\log Y = 1.8400 + 0.1970 \log X$	60
Third highest	$\log Y = 1.7720 + 0.1910 \log X$	58
Fourth highest	$\log Y = 1.5670 + 0.2370 \log X$	69
Fifth highest	$\log Y = 1.6370 + 0.1960 \log X$	75

Table 146: Salary as a Percentage of CEO's Salary

Compensation Rank	Median	Middle 50% Range Low	Middle 50% Range High
Second highest	69%	61%	82%
Third highest	55	45	65
Fourth highest	46	38	59
Fifth highest	40	36	52

Table 147: 1989 Bonus Awards (as Percent of Salary), by Company Size

Executive	Sales Volume Middle 50% Range Low $659 Million	Sales Volume Middle 50% Range Median $1.7 Billion	Sales Volume Middle 50% Range High $9.8 Billion
CEO			
1989 Bonus	52%	58%	71%
Salary	$371,000	$442,000	$609,000
Second Highest			
1989 Bonus	42%	49%	64%
Salary	$244,000	$295,000	$417,000
Third Highest			
1989 Bonus	41%	46%	55%
Salary	$201,000	$241,000	$337,000
Fourth Highest			
1989 Bonus	32%	37%	49%
Salary	$169,000	$208,000	$304,000
Fifth Highest			
1989 Bonus	31%	40%	59%
Salary	$153,000	$185,000	$260,000

Table 148: 1989 Bonus Awards

1989 Bonus Awards (Percent of Salary)	CEOS Number	CEOS Percent	Second Highest Paid Number	Second Highest Paid Percent	Third Highest Paid Number	Third Highest Paid Percent	Fourth Highest Paid Number	Fourth Highest Paid Percent	Fifth Highest Paid Number	Fifth Highest Paid Percent
100% or more	3	13%	2	8%	2	8%	1	4%	2	9%
70-99	7	29	4	17	3	12	3	13	4	17
40-69	11	46	10	42	10	40	8	35	8	35
20-39	3	13	7	29	7	28	7	30	7	30
Less than 20%	—	—	1	4	3	12	4	17	2	9
Total	24	100%	24	100%	25	100%	23	100%	23	100%
Median Bonus	60%		54%		43%		47%		46%	
Middle 50% Range	42 – 82%		34 – 68%		32 – 61%		27 – 57%		29 – 73%	

Insurance

Chart 18: Total Current Compensation of the Five Highest-Paid Executives, by Premium Income

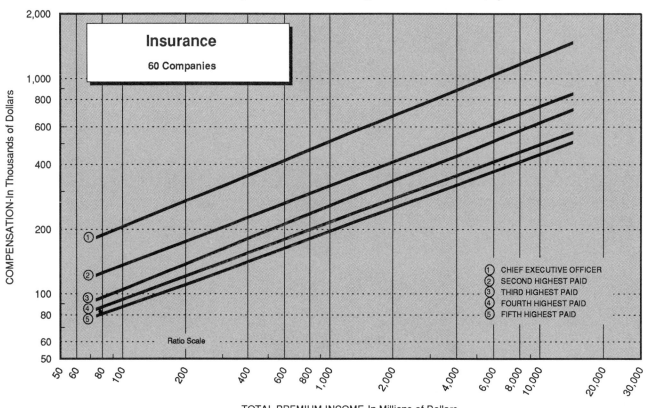

Insurance

60 Companies

COMPENSATION-In Thousands of Dollars

Ratio Scale

① CHIEF EXECUTIVE OFFICER
② SECOND HIGHEST PAID
③ THIRD HIGHEST PAID
④ FOURTH HIGHEST PAID
⑤ FIFTH HIGHEST PAID

TOTAL PREMIUM INCOME-In Millions of Dollars

Table 149: 1989 Premium Income

1989 Premium Income	Companies	
	Number	Percent
$5 billion and over	10	17%
2-4,999 billion	7	12
1-1,999 billion	9	15
500-999 million	9	15
300-499 million	8	13
200-299 million	7	12
199 million and under	10	17
Total	60	100%

Median	Middle 50% Range	
	Low	High
$583 million	$263 million	$2.9 billion

Table 150: 1989 Total Current Compensation

Compensation Rank	Median	Middle 50% Range	
		Low	High
CEO	$463,000	$318,000	$825,000
Second highest	285,000	178,000	513,000
Third highest	238,000	143,000	440,000
Fourth highest	200,000	120,000	355,000
Fifth highest	187,000	116,000	345,000

Table 151: 1989 Total Current Compensation Regression Formula

Compensation Rank	Formula	r^2
CEO	$\log Y = 1.5260 + 0.3950 \log X$	68%
Second highest	$\log Y = 1.3940 + 0.3700 \log X$	71
Third highest	$\log Y = 1.2460 + 0.3880 \log X$	73
Fourth highest	$\log Y = 1.2540 + 0.3600 \log X$	72
Fifth highest	$\log Y = 1.2230 + 0.3570 \log X$	75

Table 152: Total Current Compensation as a Percentage of CEO's Total Current Compensation

Compensation Rank	Median	Middle 50% Range	
		Low	High
Second highest	64%	56%	72%
Third highest	50	45	59
Fourth highest	44	37	51
Fifth highest	38	33	49

Table 153: 1989 Salary

Compensation Rank	Median	Middle 50% Range	
		Low	High
CEO	$350,000	$242,000	$500,000
Second highest	212,000	150,000	320,000
Third highest	185,000	124,000	262,000
Fourth highest	155,000	117,000	250,000
Fifth highest	142,000	102,000	225,000

Table 154: 1989 Salary Regression Formula

Compensation Rank	Formula	r^2
CEO	$\log Y = 1.6530 + 0.3060 \log X$	67%
Second highest	$\log Y = 1.4860 + 0.2980 \log X$	66
Third highest	$\log Y = 1.3350 + 0.3210 \log X$	73
Fourth highest	$\log Y = 1.3910 + 0.2820 \log X$	75
Fifth highest	$\log Y = 1.3380 + 0.2880 \log X$	81

Table 155: Salary as a Percentage of CEO's Salary

Compensation Rank	Median	Middle 50% Range	
		Low	High
Second highest	65%	56%	72%
Third highest	53	47	62
Fourth highest	47	40	53
Fifth highest	41	36	51

Table 156: 1989 Bonus Awards (as Percent of Salary), by Company Size

	Premium Income		
	Middle 50% Range		
	Low	Median	High
	$263	$583	$2.9
Executive	Million	Million	Billion
CEO			
1989 Bonus	31%	38%	53%
Salary	$255,000	$322,000	$517,000
Second Highest			
1989 Bonus	29%	34%	45%
Salary	$160,000	$203,000	$329,000
Third Highest			
1989 Bonus	25%	30%	40%
Salary	$131,000	$168,000	$281,000
Fourth Highest			
1989 Bonus	17%	23%	36%
Salary	$121,000	$151,000	$235,000
Fifth Highest			
1989 Bonus	17%	23%	34%
Salary	$110,000	$138,000	$218,000

Table 157: 1989 Bonus Awards

1989 Bonus Awards (Percent of Salary)	CEOS		Second Highest Paid		Third Highest Paid		Fourth Highest Paid		Fifth Highest Paid	
	Number	Percent	Number	Percent	Number	Percent	Number	Percent	Number	Percent
70% or more	11	23%	7	15%	7	16%	4	9%	3	7%
60-69	6	12	5	11	2	4%	2	4	2	4
50-59	7	14	6	13	7	16	9	20	5	11
40-49	5	10	8	17	5	11	6	13	9	20
30-39	6	12	9	19	8	18	10	22	7	16
20-29	5	10	6	13	7	16	4	9	10	22
10-19	5	10	1	2	3	7	3	7	2	4
Less than 10%	4	8	5	11	6	13	7	16	7	16
Total	49	100%	47	100%	45	100%	45	100%	45	100%
Median Bonus	49%		42%		38%		37%		35%	
Middle 50% Range	29 – 65%		29 – 61%		25 – 55%		28 – 52%		23 – 47%	

Life Insurance

Chart 19: Total Current Compensation of the Five Highest-Paid Executives, by Premium Income

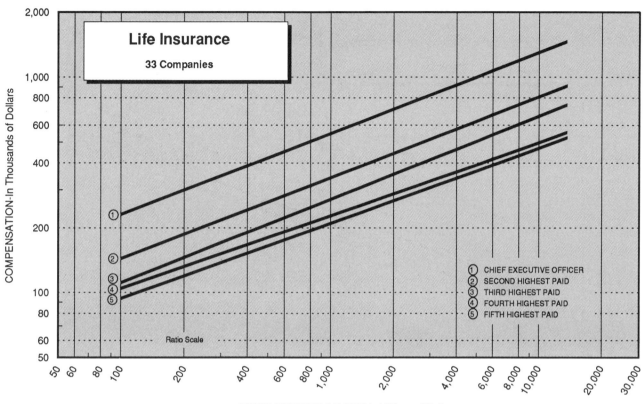

Table 158: 1989 Premium Income

1989 Premium Income	Companies Number	Companies Percent
$5 billion and over	5	15%
2-4,999 billion	4	12
1-1,999 billion	7	21
500-999 million	5	15
300-499 million	4	12
200-299 million	3	9
199 million and under	5	15
Total	33	100%

Median	Middle 50% Range Low	Middle 50% Range High
$906 million	$352 million	$2.9 billion

Table 159: 1989 Total Current Compensation Regression Formula

Compensation Rank	Formula	r^2
CEO	$\log Y = 1.6080 + 0.3770 \log X$	67%
Second highest	$\log Y = 1.3910 + 0.3800 \log X$	72
Third highest	$\log Y = 1.2820 + 0.3840 \log X$	68
Fourth highest	$\log Y = 1.3440 + 0.3380 \log X$	69
Fifth highest	$\log Y = 1.2760 + 0.3490 \log X$	73

Table 160: 1989 Salary Regression Formula

Compensation Rank	Formula	r^2
CEO	$\log Y = 1.7780 + 0.2700 \log X$	61%
Second highest	$\log Y = 1.5440 + 0.2840 \log X$	66
Third highest	$\log Y = 1.4320 + 0.2920 \log X$	66
Fourth highest	$\log Y = 1.5220 + 0.2380 \log X$	65
Fifth highest	$\log Y = 1.4360 + 0.2570 \log X$	73

Property and Casualty Insurance

Chart 20: Total Current Compensation of the Five Highest-Paid Executives, by Premium Income

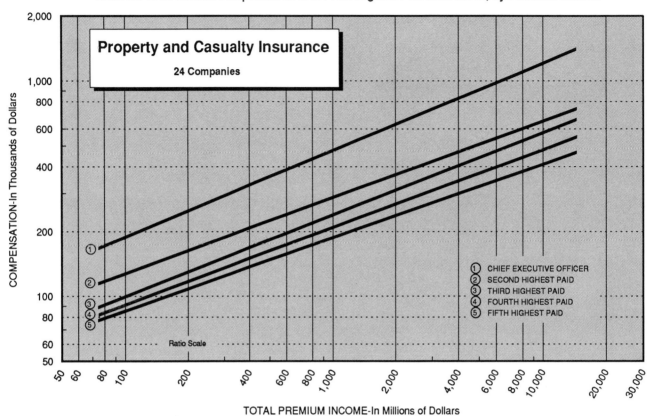

Table 161: 1989 Premium Income

1989 Premium Income	Companies Number	Companies Percent
$5 billion and over	5	21%
2-4,999 billion	2	8
1-1,999 billion	2	8
500-999 million	3	13
300-499 million	3	13
200-299 million	4	17
199 million and under	5	21
Total	24	100%

Median	Middle 50% Range Low	Middle 50% Range High
$472 million	$221 million	$2.3 billion

Table 162: 1989 Total Current Compensation Regression Formula

Compensation Rank	Formula	r^2
CEO	$\log Y = 1.4600 + 0.4060 \log X$	71%
Second highest	$\log Y = 1.4140 + 0.3490 \log X$	70
Third highest	$\log Y = 1.2310 + 0.3820 \log X$	80
Fourth highest	$\log Y = 1.2470 + 0.3580 \log X$	83
Fifth highest	$\log Y = 1.2460 + 0.3420 \log X$	84

Table 163: 1989 Salary Regression Formula

Compensation Rank	Formula	r^2
CEO	$\log Y = 1.5410 + 0.3410 \log X$	74%
Second highest	$\log Y = 1.4380 + 0.3080 \log X$	67
Third highest	$\log Y = 1.2370 + 0.3520 \log X$	81
Fourth highest	$\log Y = 1.2570 + 0.3270 \log X$	86
Fifth highest	$\log Y = 1.2370 + 0.3200 \log X$	90

Trade

Chart 21: Total Current Compensation of the Five Highest-Paid Executives, by Company Sales

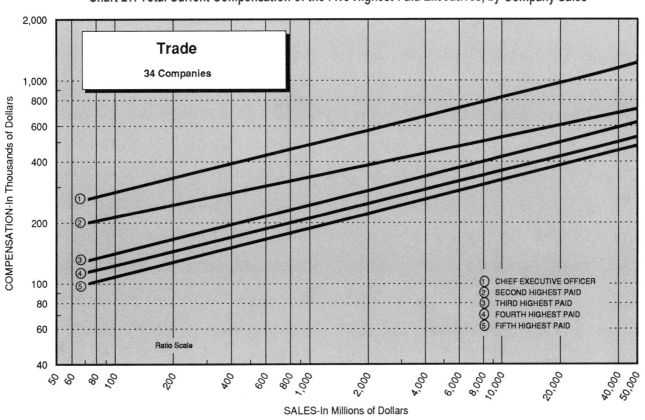

Trade

34 Companies

COMPENSATION-In Thousands of Dollars

SALES-In Millions of Dollars

Ratio Scale

① CHIEF EXECUTIVE OFFICER
② SECOND HIGHEST PAID
③ THIRD HIGHEST PAID
④ FOURTH HIGHEST PAID
⑤ FIFTH HIGHEST PAID

Table 164: 1989 Sales Volume

1989 Sales	Companies	
	Number	Percent
$5 billion and over	10	29%
2-4,999 billion	6	18
1-1,999 billion	3	9
500-999 million	6	18
300-499 million	4	12
200-299 million	—	—
199 million and under	5	15
Total	34	100%

Median	Middle 50% Range	
	Low	High
$1.6 billion	$492 million	$7.6 billion

Table 165: 1989 Total Current Compensation

Compensation Rank	Median	Middle 50% Range	
		Low	High
CEO	$520,000	$346,000	$950,000
Second highest	380,000	260,000	544,000
Third highest	257,000	183,000	395,000
Fourth highest	233,000	179,000	338,000
Fifth highest	209,000	140,000	325,000

Table 166: 1989 Total Current Compensation Regression Formula

Compensation Rank	Formula	r^2
CEO	$\log Y = 1.9910 + 0.2320 \log X$	49%
Second highest	$\log Y = 1.9350 + 0.1970 \log X$	40
Third highest	$\log Y = 1.6810 + 0.2360 \log X$	51
Fourth highest	$\log Y = 1.6300 + 0.2320 \log X$	55
Fifth highest	$\log Y = 1.5390 + 0.2430 \log X$	56

Table 167: Total Current Compensation as a Percentage of CEO's Total Current Compensation

Compensation Rank	Median	Middle 50% Range	
		Low	High
Second highest	70%	60%	82%
Third highest	50	43	66
Fourth highest	43	38	51
Fifth highest	37	32	47

Table 168: 1989 Salary

Compensation Rank	Median	Middle 50% Range	
		Low	High
CEO	$365,000	$282,000	$541,000
Second highest	260,000	225,000	380,000
Third highest	200,000	125,000	285,000
Fourth highest	182,000	125,000	230,000
Fifth highest	163,000	125,000	200,000

Table 169: 1989 Salary Regression Formula

Compensation Rank	Formula	r^2
CEO	$\log Y = 1.8230 + 0.2340 \log X$	71%
Second highest	$\log Y = 1.8040 + 0.1940 \log X$	56
Third highest	$\log Y = 1.6210 + 0.2110 \log X$	54
Fourth highest	$\log Y = 1.5160 + 0.2290 \log X$	62
Fifth highest	$\log Y = 1.5760 + 0.1960 \log X$	53

Table 170: Salary as a Percentage of CEO's Salary

Compensation Rank	Median	Middle 50% Range	
		Low	High
Second highest	71%	60%	83%
Third highest	52	49	58
Fourth highest	49	40	55
Fifth highest	43	37	51

Table 171: 1989 Bonus Awards (as Percent of Salary), by Company Size

| | Sales Volume | | |
| | Middle 50% Range | | |
Executive	Low $492 Million	Median $1.6 Billion	High $7.6 Billion
CEO			
1989 Bonus	36%	44%	54%
Salary	$285,000	$386,000	$577,000
Second Highest			
1989 Bonus	30%	38%	48%
Salary	$214,000	$271,000	$369,000
Third Highest			
1989 Bonus	29%	39%	52%
Salary	$158,000	$204,000	$284,000
Fourth Highest			
1989 Bonus	28%	33%	40%
Salary	$138,000	$183,000	$267,000
Fifth Highest			
1989 Bonus	18%	30%	47%
Salary	$130,000	$165,000	$226,000

Table 172: 1989 Bonus Awards

| 1989 Bonus Awards
(Percent of Salary) | CEOS | | Second
Highest Paid | | Third
Highest Paid | | Fourth
Highest Paid | | Fifth
Highest Paid | |
	Number	Percent	Number	Percent	Number	Percent	Number	Percent	Number	Percent
100% or more	2	7%	3	11%	3	10%	1	4%	2	8%
70-99	4	14	3	11	3	10	4	14	3	12
50-69	5	18	3	11	3	10	1	4	2	8
40-49	8	29	2	7	2	7	2	7	2	8
30-39	2	7	4	15	5	17	5	17	3	12
20-29	1	4	4	15	4	14	7	24	4	15
Less than 20%	6	21	8	30	9	31	9	31	10	39
Total	28	100%	27	100%	29	100%	29	100%	26	100%
Median Bonus	47%		37%		33%		28%		28%	
Middle 50% Range	21 – 66%		15 – 67%		17 – 57%		15 – 41%		12 – 51%	

Utilities

Chart 22: Total Current Compensation of the Five Highest-Paid Executives, by Operating Revenue

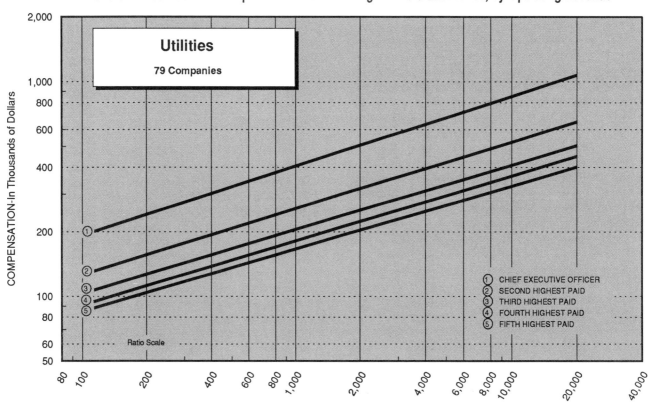

Utilities

79 Companies

COMPENSATION-In Thousands of Dollars

Ratio Scale

① CHIEF EXECUTIVE OFFICER
② SECOND HIGHEST PAID
③ THIRD HIGHEST PAID
④ FOURTH HIGHEST PAID
⑤ FIFTH HIGHEST PAID

OPERATING REVENUE-In Millions of Dollars

Table 173: 1989 Operating Revenue

1989 Operating Revenue	Companies	
	Number	Percent
$5 billion and over	12	15%
2-4,999 billion	18	23
1-1,999 billion	15	19
500-999 million	14	18
300-499 million	9	11
200-299 million	4	5
199 million and under	7	9
Total	79	100%

Median	Middle 50% Range	
	Low	High
$1.4 billion	$471 million	$3.2 billion

Table 174: 1989 Total Current Compensation

Compensation Rank	Median	Middle 50% Range	
		Low	High
CEO	$440,000	$293,000	$635,000
Second highest	297,000	176,000	415,000
Third highest	221,000	140,000	314,000
Fourth highest	184,000	124,000	282,000
Fifth highest	167,000	122,000	253,000

Table 175: 1989 Total Current Compensation Regression Formula

Compensation Rank	Formula	r^2
CEO	$\log Y = 1.6270 + 0.3270 \log X$	55%
Second highest	$\log Y = 1.4890 + 0.3080 \log X$	50
Third highest	$\log Y = 1.4130 + 0.3000 \log X$	53
Fourth highest	$\log Y = 1.3430 + 0.3050 \log X$	61
Fifth highest.............	$\log Y = 1.3340 + 0.2960 \log X$	62

Table 176: Total Current Compensation as a Percentage of CEO's Total Current Compensation

Compensation Rank	Median	Middle 50% Range	
		Low	High
Second highest	63%	57%	73%
Third highest	50	43	58
Fourth highest	44	39	52
Fifth highest	41	35	47

Table 177: 1989 Salary

Compensation Rank	Median	Middle 50% Range	
		Low	High
CEO	$345,000	$258,000	$500,000
Second highest	221,000	155,000	304,000
Third highest	173,000	128,000	243,000
Fourth highest	157,000	119,000	217,000
Fifth highest	155,000	110,000	189,000

Table 178: 1989 Salary Regression Formula

Compensation Rank	Formula	r^2
CEO	$\log Y = 1.7040 + 0.2670 \log X$	58%
Second highest	$\log Y = 1.5670 + 0.2520 \log X$	54
Third highest	$\log Y = 1.4980 + 0.2430 \log X$	58
Fourth highest	$\log Y = 1.4440 + 0.2470 \log X$	62
Fifth highest.............	$\log Y = 1.4250 + 0.2420 \log X$	65

Table 179: Salary as a Percentage of CEO's Salary

Compensation Rank	Median	Middle 50% Range	
		Low	High
Second highest	65%	59%	75%
Third highest	52	46	58
Fourth highest	47	42	55
Fifth highest	44	38	50

Table 180: 1989 Bonus Awards (as Percent of Salary), by Company Size

	Operating Revenue		
	Middle 50% Range		
	Low	Median	High
	$471	$1.4	$3.2
Executive	Million	Billion	Billion
CEO			
1989 Bonus	29%	37%	44%
Salary	$278,000	$358,000	$434,000
Second Highest			
1989 Bonus	25%	32%	38%
Salary	$185,000	$237,000	$286,000
Third Highest			
1989 Bonus	23%	31%	37%
Salary	$147,000	$187,000	$225,000
Fourth Highest			
1989 Bonus	18%	26%	32%
Salary	$133,000	$171,000	$206,000
Fifth Highest			
1989 Bonus	18%	25%	30%
Salary	$123,000	$158,000	$191,000

Table 181: 1989 Bonus Awards

1989 Bonus Awards (Percent of Salary)	CEOS		Second Highest Paid		Third Highest Paid		Fourth Highest Paid		Fifth Highest Paid	
	Number	Percent	Number	Percent	Number	Percent	Number	Percent	Number	Percent
100% or more	3	5%	2	4%	2	4%	—	—	—	—
80-99	2	3	2	4	2	4	2	4%	1	2%
60-79	6	10	3	5	2	4	3	5	3	5
50-59	7	12	8	14	4	7	2	4	2	4
40-49	10	17	4	7	6	10	5	9	6	11
30-39	6	10	10	17	12	21	13	22	11	19
20-29	12	20	13	22	12	21	9	16	12	21
10-19	11	18	12	21	13	22	16	28	14	25
Less than 10%	3	5	4	7	5	9	8	14	8	14
Total	60	100%	58	100%	58	100%	58	100%	57	100%
Median Bonus	35%		29%		28%		22%		24%	
Middle 50% Range	20 – 50%		16 – 50%		15 – 42%		15 – 39%		14 – 38%	